SINBADS
SCRAPBOOK

SINbADs
SCRAPBOOK
Secrets of a Window Cleaner
Frank Jeffery with Mal Young

BOXTREE

BROOKSIDE

In Association with Channel Four Television Corporation

First published in Great Britain in 1995
by Boxtree Limited
Text © Phil Redmond Enterprises Ltd 1995
Photographs © The Mersey Television Company Ltd 1995

12345678910

Designed by Blackjacks
Colour origination by Scanners
Printed in Great Britain by Cambus Litho Ltd

Boxtree Limited
Broadwall House
21 Broadwall
London SE1 9PL

A CIP catalogue entry for this book is available from the
British Library.

ISBN 07522 10815

Acknowledgements
The authors and publishers would like to thank the
following for their kind assistance in the preparation of
this book: Phil Redmond, Alexis Redmond, Michael
Denny, Helen Griffin, the staff and cast of Brookside
particularly Michael Starke who plays Sinbad and also
Chris Worwood at Channel 4 stills.

Front cover photograph by Trevor Owens

Photographs on p.19 by kind permission of Everton
Football Club; p.99 Liverpool Tourist Board/Merseyside
Photo Library and p.101 Aero Films

CONTENTS

INTRODUCTION
to me scrapbook
© me, 1996

Bet you didn't think I kept a scrapbook, did you? I don't broadcast it, like, because some people might think it's what trainspotters do. But I found this big book on a tip once, not long after I first started me window round on Brookside. I was having a bit of a thin time, in a manner of ~~speaking~~ speaking, and you can sometimes make a few bob sifting through other people's unconsidered trifles . . . Cast-offs, I mean not the kind with jelly and custard.

So I started pasting in odds and ends, scraps of this and that. You know memories and that . . . Snapshots, newspapers cuttings, football programmes, that sort of thing. I did it to keep a sort of record of me life in a place that seemed to get more important to me as time went by.

yours truly

me as Winston (but I'm a bit too thin)

After a time, the scrapbook got to be a sort of diary, with me putting down what was going on in the Close. I'm not claiming to be that Samual Pepys feller, but some of it tells you quite a lot about me mates and neighbours.

When I took a look through the book I realised it told quite a lot about Brookside Close . . . in fact more than about just me! I've worked and lived around the Close for more than ten years now and believe me if anyone knows what's going on it's the window cleaner. You ask yours, you'll be surprised. You can't see behind closed doors but through panes of glass it's a different story. Not that I'm nosy, like . . . just interested in people. You know . . . people watching.

Brookside's like any other place, of course. People come and go, they get mad at each other, they fall out . . ., sometimes even have fights. They fall in love and fall out again regularly.

Some of them have kids and having kids means having problems, as any parent will tell you. I never knew me Mum till just a couple of years ago, but I do understand what it's like bringing kids up.

We've had our fair share of drama on the close . . . - a gunman holding three people hostage, fires, robberies, all kinds of iron girder . . . that's murder to you . . . but if you don't mind I won't talk about murder just yet . . . I'll leave that till later . . . but through all this, the residents just went on living their own lives. One of the more interesting Sunday papers - I won't say scandalous - used to have a slogan that said ALL HUMAN LIFE IS THERE. Well that's nothing when you start to look through me scrapbook and see what's been going on in the close over the years . . .

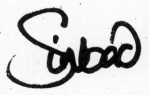

SINBAD'S

SCOUSE SPEAK

Much has been said, good and bad, about the Liverpool accent. Well, I just want to put the record straight that we talk dead proper, like. If anyone tells you otherwise just tell them to go and listen to someone from Birmingham, Newcastle or Devon. A lot of people, who've never visited Liverpool or think it's like an episode of Bread, think we all go round cracking gags and calling each other wack!

It might have been true a long time ago but if you called someone wack or wacker now he'd give you a very funny look. As if you were taking the St Michael. (It's supposed to come from horsewhacker, a feller who leads horses, from the days when Liverpool folk weren't supposed to be skilled enough to do much else.)

Anyway I've written down a couple or three Scouse expressions for you. Learn them and you could get instant street cred in my city. Or instant Close cred in Brookside. Everyone knows <u>Scouse</u>, or <u>Scouser</u> means someone from Liverpool. It comes from our famous stew. The one I've given the recipe for in my ~~xext~~ section on cookery.

One of the things we do is shorten words and tack a Y sound on the end. It's to save time cause we're always dead busy. <u>Offy</u> means off-licence, for instance, and <u>ozzy</u> means hospital, but don't confuse the two. Though I have known one or two who spent so much time going down the offy they ended up in the ozzy. Suffering from what I have heard called <u>Sir Roses of the liver</u>.

You'll notice the H has gone missing from hospital. Cockneys aren't the only people who can drop their aitches. Liverpool 'olds the Cup, you might say.

Sometimes the Y ending can make a word longer, add an extra syllable. Best comes out as <u>bezzy</u>, as in "Jimmy Corkhill's me bezzy mate." Though that situation's changed recently.

<u>Sagging</u> means staying off school or work, what other places might call wagging or bunking off.

<u>Made up</u> means pleased. You'll often hear someone say "I'm made up for you about your new job." On second thoughts you don't hear that often. <u>Chuffed</u> means about the same.

<u>Loads</u> means loads of grief or aggro, as in "They're giving me loads at work."

first-mate
Jimmy Corkhill,
now
demoted.

DD Dixon used to be in a convent, but Ron was having nun of that...

Religion has always been a big thing to talk about in Liverpool, so it's not surprising we've got our own vocabulary. A Catholic (or cat lick) can be a <u>candle</u> (from roman candle, the firework) a <u>rat catcher</u> (RC again) or an <u>ailmary</u> or even a <u>left-footer</u>. There are fewer words for Protestant: <u>prot, prod, proddy</u> and that's about it. A monastery is a <u>monkey house</u> and a nunnery or convent a <u>penguin's palace</u>, because nuns are supposed to look like penguins in their black habits with the white bits. Mind you, modern nuns with their short skirts and Vauxhall Corsas don't look much like the bird on the biscuit to me. Actually I'd heard Ron Dixon's estranged missus, DD, used to be a nun – but Ron was having 'nun' of it ...!

Oh and a synagogue is called a <u>sinner club</u> by some people.

And I have heard a rabbi called a <u>dicky-docker</u>, though that's a bit of a rude one. Not one you'd repeat to Pat Farnham.

Policemen used to be called <u>scuffers</u> in Liverpool – could be something to do with scuffles, apparently, or even the cuffs they put on wrongdoers. But nowadays everyone calls them the <u>bizzies</u>, from busy-bodies. Though a <u>busy lizzie</u> is a gossipy old woman. There's a few of those in Brookside, and I don't just mean Julia Brogan. Another word for the likes of her is <u>owld biddy</u>.

Julia Brogan doesn't always look like an owld biddy.

<u>Cop</u> or <u>cop off</u> means to get off with a member of the other sex, and nothing to do with the Kop. But it has been known during the more boring matches.

A kid can also cop for punishment at school.

<u>Dead</u> in Liverpool usually just means very. <u>Dead Andy</u> isn't a bloke waiting for the undertaker: it's just a phrase meaning very useful. An undertaker, by the way, can be called a boxer - he pops you in the box - or Ernie. He's the one who gives you the urn.

<u>Sound</u> means perfect and <u>ace</u> or <u>brill</u> mean about the same. <u>Cracker</u> doesn't just mean Jimmy's soft dog; it also means great. <u>Gobsmacked</u> means startled - as if you've had a smack in the gob.

A <u>yuppy yappy</u> is a pedigree dog and a <u>yuppy puppy</u> is a young pedigree dog. Jimmy Corkhill's Cracker qualifies - he's a Staffordshire bull terrier - though no-one would think of Jim as a yuppy owner. Except himself. I think he won it in a bet or got it for a debt or something. A family tree wasn't included, but there's no doubt Cracker's got a touch of nobility.

The <u>Echo</u> means the Liverpool Echo, our famous newspaper. "I seen it in the Echo" means it must be true.

<u>Leg off</u> is a funny phrase. Nothing to do with leg over, or amputations, it just means a lot, or excessively. As in "I was crying me leg off." It's also something Jimmy does a lot if the Bizzies are after him - he legs off, he does one - in other words, he runs off very quickly!

Rhyming slang isn't confined to the Old Kent Road, any more than aitch-disposal. The normal Liverpool word for trousers is <u>kecks</u>. (They say it comes from sailor talk. The old merchant seamen called them kicks but ashore in Liverpool the word got corrupted. As did many of the merchant seamen when they went down Lime Street.)

If you hear a bloke talking about his <u>Gregories</u> he means his trousers. From Gregory Peck - rhymes with keck. But <u>Gregory Peck</u> also means neck in Scouse rhyming slang, so "Do that again and I'll break your Gregory!" doesn't mean I'll rip your jeans.

An <u>iron</u> is a gay bloke, because iron hoof rhymes with poof. You'll probably recall the old Scaffold song Thank You Very Much, which includes the line Thank you very much for the Aintree Iron, generally thought to mean the late Brian Epstein, who came from that posh part of Liverpool. He's the one who said the Beatles would be bigger than Elvis and it turned out True. <u>Iron</u> can also mean trouble - as in "There'll be iron

girder" - murder!

<u>Jockeys</u> means chips, from jockeys' whips. <u>On the Nat</u> means on the social. You know, Nat King Cole rhymes with dole.

<u>One of Lewis's</u> is a phrase you'll sometimes hear and it means someone stood really still. Lewis's is one of our department stores.

It comes from the window dummies, who don't usually have too much to say for themselves. "He was stood standing there like one of Lewis's," means he was a bit gormless, couldn't rise to the occasion.

Lewis's has a big male nude statue over the main entrance and he's known as <u>Dicky Lewis</u>. From which you'll work out that he's well-endowed. Feller called Jacob Epstein made it, they say, though I don't think he was local. Not related to Brian at any rate.

If you hear kids talking about kicking a <u>Casey</u> it doesn't mean they're being racist about the Irish. The word just means football, from the old lace-up case ones. <u>The lecky</u> means electricity: "I can't pay me lecky bill" is a phrase I've heard too often. If you have a coin-in-the-slot lecky meter it's called <u>the mint</u>, because it's full of coins. I remember a sound fella, used to live at Number 10 well before Mandy moved in, called Billy Corkhill. He was a spark, an electrician, who, rumour had it fixed his lecky meter so he didn't have to pay .... Got a terrible <u>shock</u> when his bill came through ....

<u>Our kid</u> means a brother or sister. The posh word is sibling, I think, but I've never heard anyone say our sibling. Maybe they do in yuppy households like Lord and Lady Farnham.

Lord & Lady Farnham with the heir to the Brookside estate.

Bevvy means drink and bevvied drunk, something I've been on the odd occasion. I'm only a sociable drinker. Trouble is I'm very sociable. Scally brings us back to Jimmy. It means a scallywag, of course.

Avvy means afternoon, Crimbo means Christmas. If someone's a bit slow on the uptake you might just say "He still believes in Daddy Crimbo."

A pair of bills means underpants. Comes from the tellyman Bill Grundy who became dead well-known after his run-in with the Sex Pistols. Grundies rhymes with Undies.

German swines means my shoe size, nines. Jimmy Corkhill asks if any garden gates have fallen off lorries lately. Eights.

Go 'ead is a phrase outsiders have trouble with, but it just means go ahead. Have your say, old chap.

Scran means food but nobody quite knows why. Not even Bing. Off his cake means doo-lally, a bit silly, like.

Cream-crackered means knackered, done in, and deffo means definitely. After a day's window cleaning I'm deffo cream-crackered, especially if I'd to deal with a nasty Ally, or alsatian dog.

I'll leave you with the most famous Liverpool word for goodbye. 'Tarra.'

I've never really been much of a romancer. I'm not backwards at coming forward like, but I can't be a smoothy with the women. What the old Liverpool fellers called a Rhubarb Vasselino, that's something I could never manage to be.

I prefer to use me shy, retiring routine. I've heard girls love the quiet ones. And when I crack me scrim on me window round, I drive the housewives into a frenzy.

I'd been in love a couple of times before I met Mandy Jordache. The first time – the first time I really knew it was the big one (or so I thought at the time) – was with Caroline Choi.

She was a beautiful girl from Hong Kong and she didn't want to know about me. Not romantically, anyway.

She turned up in the Close with her brother, Dr Michael Choi, in May 1989. They moved into Number 7 and the first time I saw her I thought I'd been hit by a thunderbolt. Me shammy went all limp.

She had this jewellery business, making junk earrings and such like. Though it wasn't junk, really. Some of it was really good gear. Anyway she said I could help her make it and I was over the seven moons of Saturn.

Other fellers declare their love with flowers and chocolates, I cleaned her windows for free in a grand, romantic gesture. But she could never see me as more than a mate, could Caroline. She was besotted with a right smooth-talking supersmarm called James Markham. He'd been an old boyfriend and he turned up again with his flash car, flash clothes and flash manners, just as I was starting to flash me pearly whites.

It was a wonder he wasn't arrested for flashing.

Of course he had to help Caroline on the business side – I was only good enough to put together a pair of earrings – and before long he was helping himself to her cash. He had a yen for that sort of thing, or is that Japanese? She discovered the fraud but didn't at first believe it was him.

Not her St James – he couldn't behave like that. Finally she worked out that he'd done it because he was deeper in debt than the British Exchequer.

There were some fairly nasty characters xxxxxx chasing after James for his other villainies and he took off from Liverpool fast.

Eventually we got news he'd been killed in a car crash in Aberdeen and that the Macbizzies thought it was murder.

Couldn't have happened to a nicer man.

I thought with Flash James out of the way Caroline might have some time for me, but it was as if I didn't exist. She packed up and went back to Hong Kong. Her brother Michael, who'd fallen in love with a scientist called Alison Gregory, took off for the States with her. Caroline had been here less than a year.

They say you never forget your first big love and I'll never forget Caroline. Though I doubt she remembers me. I heard she got married in Hong Kong a couple of years ago.

But I'm a great believer in fate and it obviously wasn't meant to be. And besides, I wouldn't have gone through me next two big romances if Caroline had realised just what a catch I am – her loss.

love
incarnate

Soccer

As everyone knows, Liverpool is a football town. It has two Premier League teams based just a couple of hundred yards apart: Liverpool FC at Anfield, Everton FC at Goodison Park.

The late Bill Shankley, Liverpool manager once said: "There are two football teams in Liverpool. Liverpool and Liverpool Reserves." The Blues forgave him the joke, though one or two hotheads at Goodison Park were all for burning him in effigy.

Bill was also the man who was once asked if football was a matter of life or death to him. "Oh, no," he said, "it's much more important than that." Actually, once Bill spoke to me in a pub near the ground . . . he said "Eh, get out the way, fatty, I wanna get to the bar."

The entire city supports one team or the other. Nobody supports both. It's nothing really to do with religion these days . . . Proddies, Left Footers, Jews, Muslims, Buddhists, atheists and How's yer Fathers, turn up at both grounds in gobsmacking numbers. It's nothing to do with which part of Liverpool you come from either. If you took a street and

a happy moment

knocked at every house you'd probably find equal numbers of fans for each side.

It's got quite a lot to do with family loyalty. If your old man was Liverpool you're sure to follow him. Likewise if he went to Everton.

I was brought up in a children's home. so I'm not sure how I became an Evertonian. Knowing my luck me dad was probably a Man United supporter. These days I suppose you'd say I'm a lapsed Evertonian, since I don't get to the match too often. There are just too many things to do.

I do know one thing, though. My kids will support blue-and-white Everton against red Liverpool forever.

I won't teach them to; it'll be genetic - in the blood . . .

Of course Everton's sacred ground, Goodison Park, was the place I proposed to Marcia Barrett, on the electronic scoreboard.

Not just because I was an Everton fan, but because I cleaned the windows of a couple of the players. They saw their way clear through their windows and then saw my way clear to the lit-up proposal.

Sort of gave a shine to the whole affair. Not that it got me anywhere . . . she jibbed me a few weeks later . . . maybe she was a rugby fan . . .?

What the well-dressed footballer wears at Goodison Park. Never know why they call it a strip, though they sometimes take their shirts off at the end.

I used to have this daydream in which Mandy and I open up a small business. Nothing fancy, like maybe a cafe like the ones you used to get on the old dock road, though the few of those left have gone a bit upmarket lately. They used to be full of brill characters, great atmosphere and even better scran . . . (that's food to you posh ones).

I could see Mandy smiling at the customers and fetching their scran with me in the kitchen cooking it.

There is only one snag. I can only cook two dishes and that's it. I've no time for that new vile cuisine - five leaves in a poncy picture on your plate and nothing to eat.

But I do a first class Scouse, Liverpool's famous stew, and I produce the best egg and chips this side of Manchester.

A really perfect egg and chips will cheer up anyone. I used to make it to bring Mandy out of one of her depressions. And there were times when she had plenty to be depressed about.

Liverpudlians have been called Scousers for a hundred years and more because of that stew but it didn't actually originate in the city, or so know-all David 'Bing' Crosbie told me. Though he had to look it up himself in some reference book in the Central Library in William Brown Street. The merchants sailors used to make a stew of meat, any vegetables they had aboard and crushed ships biscuit.

For some reason this was called Lobscouse. Even Bing can't tell me why. When they brought it ashore in Liverpool the name got shortened to Scouse. These days we forget the ships biscuit; otherwise it's much the same.

There are three main versions: Blind Scouse which you make when you can't afford meat (one for the trendy veggies!), Basic Scouse which uses cheap stewing steak and Posh Scouse which uses the finest leg of Welsh lamb.

p'haps sometimes I could do with a bit more exercise

Le Café Sinbad

Oeuf sur le plat avec frites

***

Ragout d'agneau Scouse

***

Pain Sunblest, beurre de Nouvelle-Zelande

Boisson (the) et service compris 25 francs.

English money accepted.

Basic Scouse Recipe

(serves four)

1lb stewing steak
1lb potatoes
½lb carrots
2 onions
1½ Oxo cubes made into stock with 1 pint of water
a little vegetable oil

Dust the cubed meat with seasoned flour and seal it in the oil with the chopped onions in a large saucepan.

Add the carrots and Oxo stock and simmer for 20 minutes. Add the potatoes and cook gently for a further 40 minutes, or 60 if you like a thick stew, but don't let it burn. Add more water if you need to.

For Blind Scouse leave out the meat and double the quantity of potatoes and carrots.

For Posh Scouse use a leg of lamb instead of stewing steak, marinade it with herbs and some red wine for a couple of hours. Arrange the meat and vegetables in a casserole in layers, add chicken stock rather than Oxo and cook in a moderate oven for about an hour and a half.

Me mate, Mick Johno, runs the local pizza parlour . . . he's a good man, and a great cook, trained up years ago - the lot . . . but I'm not bad meself when it comes to the old culinary skills.

Not too many people know how I became Brookside's champion egg and chips cook. I had this mate Dave who owned one of those old cafes on the Dock Road.

Dave learned to cook in some big hotel. He slaved away there doing breakfasts and the feller who taught him was a right hard case. Every time Dave mucked up a fried egg this chef made him eat it. Stood over him while he forked in every last burned or gooey mouthful. After half a dozen fried eggs, it starts to have some funny effects on your body, so Dave learned the right way.

This is the method he taught me when I used to give him a hand in the kitchen occasionally.

Use a good vegetable oil, not too much of it, get it hot in the frying pan, then take it off the heat. Break the egg into the pan and let it settle. Turn down the heat before bringing back the pan and let the egg cook fairly slowly. Towards the end use a spoon or one of those fancy slices to flip some of the hot oil over the yolk, to give it a milky look.

<u>Serve it fast.</u>

Of course you have to have your chips ready. Dave taught me the perfect method, which I admit does take a bit of time and fuss. I have been known to take a packet of crinkle-cuts straight out the freezer, though I'd be glad if you kept that between ourselves.

The perfect way starts with selecting the perfect spud . . . a good decent size, you want and then cutting you chips to near enough equal size, drying them with kitchen paper. You then part-cook them in hot oil, drain them and let them rest for a bit. I often take a bit of a rest myself at this stage, feet up with a cup of tea.

Then when you're ready to get the oil really hot and fry the little beggers again till they're crisp and golden. A very important finishing touch is to drain the chips and then salt them while they're still in the pan and there go - chip á la Sinbad.

If all this seems too much like hard work you could always go down the Dock Road for your egg and chips. Say Sinbad sent you.

If I ever do get started in a little cafe of me own I'd like the menu just egg and chips and Scouse, with tea and bread and butter of course, for the finishing touch. Eh, I'm telling you - it'd be a right little goldmine. Maybe me dream will come true one day, and I'll put that Maxie Farnham out of business, with his over posh and over priced Grant's Restaurant. I could even get his wife, Pat to do the menu in French for us - add a bit of class, like.

Sinbad's Sartorial Elegance

If there was ever a competition for the best-dressed man on Brookside Close I wouldn't bet on me winning it. I might risk a few bob on coming last though, but I wouldn't spend me winnings on clothes. Like the late Frank Rogers used to say "As long as it's clean and warm, it'll do me." Straight talking man was Frank.

I've seen Jimmy Corkhill in some pretty sharp suede and leather jackets over the years - although I don't ask what lorry they fell off. Max Farnham thinks he looks dead suave in his flash suits but I think he just looks a right poser. On the whole Brookside isn't exactly the North West's centre for male fashion. I mean - have you seen the state of Ron Dixon since he's been knocking about with his young floosie, Bev - he's been dressing as if he's a teenager, not the local grocer.

Mandy is always on at me to smarten up a bit and I do make an effort for her. Like I change me jeans for a clean pair of jeans, if I'm taking her out. Put on a denim shirt maybe. Even a denim jacket. I like denim - it's well, sort of functional and always in fashion. Problem is, I start looking like something out of Bonanza.

Otherwise me uniform for window cleaning, or working as shop's caretaker is a pair of jeans, a tee-shirt or sweatshirt and comfy trainers. With thermals for winter, I've got the perfect, all year round wardrobe for every occasion. Although, during the winter months, you do work up a sweat on the windows, and I have been known to strip down to me kecks - topless, so to speak. Problem is I've been ordered by Bing's resident committee to cover up, XXX cause I was driving the housewives wild.

Like a lot of locals I buy me clothes down the Greaty, a street market off the Scotty Road. Its proper name is the Great Homer Street Market and you can but most things there. I've bought a few things off Jimmy Corkhill over the XXXX years . . . He says they're factory seconds, but who needs a sweatshirt with only one armhole? A one-armed bandit, maybe? Anyway, Jimmy used to do a nice line in designer T-shirts. I bought a couple of what I thought were dead smart Lacoste ones off him - dirt cheap. I was made up with them, until Maxie Farnham pointed out the logo was supposed to be a crocodile, not a Himalayan yak!

Anyway I'm of the opinion that all clothes are designer clothes. They didn't make themselves did they? Somebody must have designed them. Like all singing is folk singing: have you ever heard a horse warble?

I do own one dead smart double-breasted blue suit for special occasions - weddings, funerals and unfortunately, of late, court appearances. A couple of polyester ties picked up cheap because who wants to make poor little silkworms munch away on mulberry leaves forever for something you only wear twice a year?

I've got one white shirt that's got a bit tight about the collar since I bought it. Shrinkage. Honest . . .

Casually dressed for the heat of Spain. Barry & Terry were jealous of me shorts.

Me wearing the robes of me Profession.

Actually, I'm really made up with me suit - I love wearing it, makes me feel good . . . you know, dead powerful, like Mike Douglas' character in Wall St. It's pure wool, you know (I've never quite understood this pure wool thing. Does it come from sheep that think only pure thoughts? And what do they do with all the impure wool? I'm always thinking things like that . . . Like in French restaurants where they have frogs legs - what do they do with all the frogs bodies?)

finally a
T-Shirt
that fits!

The Trouble with Jimmy

by Sinbad

There are people who will tell you the Corkhill brothers – Jimmy and Billy – almost turned Brookside into Crookside. And there's some truth in it. Basically Billy seemed the straighter of the two. A good family man, who's wife Doreen liked to go out on dates a lot with her flexible friend. Gave him some big financial headaches. So who could blame him for fiddling his leccy meter or getting involved with the odd dodgy deal courtesy of his brother Jimmy.

Jimmy had done time years ago – breaking and entering, nothing he considers too serious. I'd have put Jim down as a small-time user-friendly crim – well, I would, wouldn't I, since we were mates for so long – until he started taking drugs and dealing in them. I can't give the Sinbad seal of approval to a man who sells smack to kids, which Jim does.

He got into it when he was guest bouncer at Barry Grant's disco-nightclub on the Parade, La Luz.

Confiscated some Ecstasy from a couple of kids and tried it out for a laugh. Waste not, want not. Actually I think the divvy did it as a dare. Before that Jim had taken nothing stronger than regular overdoses of bevvy. After that he saw himself as a pioneer experimenter in illegal substances.

I feel sorry for him, but I can't really forgive him the drugs thing. And he's done a couple of other things to me personally that a mate shouldn't do to a mate.

Like selling his "story" to the Press for a grand when me and Mandy were brought back from Ireland. Like when Mandy was waiting for the verdict at her murder trial and Jim tried to get me to sell him and Jackie Number 10. Because I wouldn't need all that space in a four-bedroom house with Mandy and Beth doing time, would I? After all, they'd have their own self-contained cell and en-suite.

Billy – the elder brother – is out of the Brookside frame these days. He married Sheila Grant, from across the road, and went off to live in Basingstoke, wherever that is. Billy cleaned up his act cause of Sheila, and Jimmy says he's straight as a die, these days.

But I'd bet money slightly curved would be a better description. It's easier for a corkscrew to go straight than a Corkhill. Except for Billy's son Rod, who became a bizzie and brought shame on all the Corkhills as the white sheep of the family. Billy must have wondered if he was the lad's true father.

I suppose Billy's hairdresser daughter Tracy made up for it by taking up with a real hard man, for a while, Barry Grant. Fortunately, for Billy's blood pressure, it didn't last.

Anyway, I'm trying to tell you about Jimmy. In spite of everything you can't help liking him. He *enjoys* his villainy so much, does Jim. He's got this big satisfied smile as he tells you about a scam he's pulled, or plans to pull.

He really throws himself wholeheartedly into villainy. You have to admire a man who enjoys his work so much. Pity he's not very good at it.

All right, in the early days I was right there with him, though I was much too scared to have any part of his wilder crimes. Like robbing a jeweller's on a

Barry Grant, Brookside's hard man who could sometimes be a bit of a softy.

motorbike. Or really dangerous stuff like squatting in one of Barry Grant's shops and opening up Kowboy Kutz to sell bent gear. Barry reckoned Jimmy owed him two thousand quid in rent, not a position I'd like to be in. I wouldn't sleep nights owing two bob to Barry. But Jim came out of it alive, though Barry blew up Kowboy Kutz or so the rumour goes. Barry said it was a gas leak, but he had that look on his face.

Jim got away with most things until he was so far into drugs he was burgling half the Close to support the habit. Of course the bizzies caught him, helped by steady Eddie Banks, and of course he did the Monopoly. Do not pass go. Go straight to jail. Got nine months.

Where he learned a lot more about drugs and drug dealing. "They're easier to get in here than outside," he told me once with that satisfied grin. I was doing half a Monopoly – just visiting jail. Like a fool I slipped Jim a tenner saying it wasn't to be used for drugs. I'd bet another tenner it was.

But Jim told his wife Jackie he was clean inside and wouldn't go back to smack, coke, heroin, uppers, downers, junior aspirin or Smarties. She believed him, which was surprising, since she had a talent for catching Jim out. He'd taken a gold bracelet she had and their insurance policies to make £2,000 for a drug deal. She found out and in the end he did get the bracelet back for her.

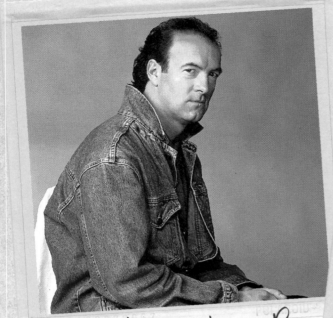

Jimmy as he sees himself:
a hard man in soft denim.

A board meeting of
CorkSin Enterprises.

Jim in his element –
selling stolen goods
from a shop!

Togetherness, Corkhill-style. Soon after this Jackie threw Jim out again. He probably made her pay the bill.

She'd even caught him snorting coke or something and had flushed the stuff down the loo. But still she believed him when he was inside and saying he hated drugs now. I suppose she felt sorry for him.

She loves him in a funny sort of way. They first met in a pub in 1971 when she was a teenager and he wasn't much more. He noticed her because she was wearing extra tight white jeans – probably wanted to find out which lorry they fell off – and they got married pretty young. But like everyone who got married in the early 70's, they can't show their photo album – remember the flares, the platforms and the collars?

Been wed for well over 20 years now – off and on. They tend to break up and go off with other people (well he does) and then get drawn back together. They've both got terrible tempers, so they shout and scream at each other and she throws things and then next day they're all lovey-dovey again. I suppose it suits some people, that. Life isn't dull, like.

When Jim came out of jail he found Ron Dixon's feet under Jackie's table and Jackie's feet under Ron's duvet, or so Jim thought. Ron's wife DD had gone off and Ron had tried to seduce Jackie, who was working as one of his shop assistants, in the stockroom of the Trading Post.

She knocked Ron back, but she still gave him a roof over his head. There was murder, with first Ron being thrown out by Jimmy, then Jackie threw Jimmy out for even thinking it!

Ron tried but Jackie knocked him back. Said there were limits to her duties at the Trading Post.

Then the old Corkhill magnet worked again and Jim and Jackie reunited. Ron took up with the young Bev, which seemed a great cop to him at the time but has brought middle-aged second thoughts.

No, I'm not going off at a tangerine or something again. The connection with Jim is that Bev's elder sister Lyn married Frank Rogers. And on their wedding day Frank got stuck into the champagne and gave Lyn and Tony Dixon a ride in the hired Rolls.

Crashed into a car driven by Jimmy. If Frank was half-cut on champagne, Jim was on coke, higher than Richard Branson's balloon. Frank was killed. Spent his honeymoon in the cemetery. Leaving Lyn a widow with a wedding cake for company. Little Tony Dixon was in a coma for a while, but eventually died. Jimmy gave up the drugs.

But Jimmy's still heavily into dealing, though technically he's employed as a sort of dogsbody back at La Luz. Never got his old security job back there. Just recently he bought a cab company as a cover and a way of explaining the drug profits away to any bizzie who wants to know. He even bought Number 10 off me with his ill-gotten profits. Him and Jackie have firmly put their stamp on it.

The funny thing is although I can't forgive the drugs business, I can forgive him all those earlier scams, tricks, cons and crimes, in some of which I was involved anyway.

But I could never quite see the value of his work as an insurance burglar. First he broke into his own brother Billy's house by prior arrangement, so debt-ridden Billy could collect a few quid from the premium pedlars. But Jim did so much damage – making it look good, he said – that Billy lost out on the deal.

Second time – and I would have been personally involved in this meself if I hadn't bottled out – he did a good job robbing Mick Johnson's place to give Mick a windfall.

Except it turned out Mick wasn't insured.

A little detail we should have checked on first. And would have done if Mick knew what we were on about. But then if Mick had known he wouldn't have let us do it. Some people are too honest for their own good.

I've seen Jim scared a few times, though most of the time he's got more bottle than HP Sauce. But I've never seen him so shaken as the time he thought he'd got AIDS. He'd been using needles that might have been used before for his drug stuff and a clinic advised him to have an AIDS check.

Just go and be sure, like. Well Jim didn't want to know and then he got sick and thought the AIDS had got him.

Turned out to be chickenpox. He was RIR positive. For Rhode Island Red.

His dealings with the medical profession have always been a bit unusual. He had to give a sample once and didn't fancy it, so he turned up with a little bottle that was actually dog's pee.

Came from his Staffordshire bull terrier Cracker.

When the sample was analysed they reckoned Jim had distemper. Wonder they didn't whip him into ozzy as the first recorded human case. Of course if Cracker had been a bitch he might have shown up as pregnant. If that happened he'd have sold his story to the tabloids for sure.

Jimmy's got two kids: Lindsey, who didn't want him at her wedding – she probably thought the father of the bride might nick the church candlesticks while the vicar wasn't looking – and Jimmy Junior, who never got on with his father.

In fact he told mum Jackie how he'd seen Jim in bed with her sister Val when he was eight and caused one of Jackie's walkouts. At least Jimmy Senior's never been a grass. And he got round Jackie in the end.

Cracker: a most unusual specimen.

Well, Lindsey had something to do with that. She told Jim to make an effort to get back with her Mum. And Jackie was in a good mood because Lindsey had just told her she was pregnant.

That was a stroke of the Corkhill luck. No matter what happens somebody up there seems to be looking after Jim.

I'll bet when he dies he'll knock on the Golden Gates and they'll let him in because they've mislaid the incriminating documents.

Or Jim has fixed it with somebody.

The farnham - Dixon FEUD

All in all the residents have pretty well got on with each other on Brookside Close. Alright, there might have been the odd little difference of opinion .... well, okay, disagreements, then ..... Yeah, I know <u>and</u> the odd murder or three. But apart from that we're all just one big happy Residents Association under our glorious leader, Bing.

Actually, now I come to think of it, maybe things aren't so rosy in the garden, or the living rooms, for that matter.

I suppose the biggest fall out I've witnessed since Chernobyl has been the long running feud between the Lord and Lady Farnham and their next door neighbours, the Dixons. And as if that wasn't bad enough, they're now neighbours at the shops as well as the Close.

To understand the war of the posers, you have to understand the families involved. They both arrived, lock stock and gun barrel, on the Close in October 1990 and war was declared within hours.

Now, as window cleaner and shops caretaker, who else but me to have such a vantage point to watch the sparks fly. At times, I've felt like one of those umpires at Wimbledon - New balls please!

Right from the off you couldn't have found two more different families. Ron Dixon had been working in a factory in Kirkby - before he got the old heave-ho, made redundant and bought a mobile shop with his paper handshake.

Actually, Ron got the idea for his Meals on Wheels from the town of Kirkby itself. Back in the late fifties when they were moving loads of people out from the inner city, round Scotty Road, to the new, green promised land, they forgot one thing - shops. Thousands of people moving into their new town, but only six shops. The queues must have put Russia to shame.

Anyway, as usual, the old entrepreneurial spirit came to the fore, and before long old post office vans, ambulances, anything with four wheels and half an engine was being converted into a mobile shop, taking the goods to the customers.

And so it came to pass, in October 1990, the day the Farnhams were just happily settling in to their cosy new home. Suddenly the peace was shattered by the noisy arrival of the Dixons' Moby, all loaded up with furniture, and even an old bath strapped to the roof. It looked like the start of the Beverly Hill Billies Show, but before you could say Buddy Ebson, Maxie and

The sight that struck fear into the farnhams. Ron, DD + brood with the dreaded Moby.

Pat were out to greet them. "What have we done to deserve this?" uttered Max, as his chin scraped on the ground. The Moby uttered it's own hello's with a touch of chronic flatulence, backfiring so loudly nearly every window on the Close shattered and could have put me out of a job. For Max and Ron it was hate at first sight.

The Dixon clan (or as Maxie christened them, the Clampettes) poured out of the Moby onto the Close, ready to make their mark on the place. And what a mark. There was all kinds all over the front garden - old one-armed bandits, baths, doors - anything and everything. It looked like a street market in Calcutta. Now some people collect stamps or butterflies - but not Ron. He collected bric-a-brac. Always on the lookout for a bargain, something he could sell for a quick profit. He saw Number 8 Brookside Close as his very own Trump Towers. And he always carried his own bible in his back pocket - the latest copy of the Merseymart free newspaper .... Full of bargains and, in Ron's eyes, potential loot.

His wife DD was quite different to Ron. A lot quieter, and easy going. Her real name's Deborah, but DD just sounded more friendly. I just thought she had a stutter. She seemed to have Ron a bit under the thumb, and was always on at him to tidy up his mess. I suppose we should have seen then that the marriage wouldn't last, but who knows what goes on behind people's front doors?
She also had a job and a half keeping their kids under control. Mike, the eldest lad, Jackie (who later started spelling her name Jacqui for some reason!) and a right little tearaway, young Tony.

DD Dixon. I thought her first name was a stutter.

The Dixons had well and truly arrived. The Farnhams weren't sure whether to barricade themselves in or run for the hills!

The Farnhams were a totally different kettle of fish. The kettle was silver - well, silver plate - and the fish was probably smoked salmon. A pair of yuppies if ever I saw one. Patricia was in PR and advertising, that sort of thing. Always swanning about in smart, expensive outfits. At first I thought she'd be a bit snooty, but I have to admit, once I got to know her, she was alright. Even managed to cadge the odd cuppa out of her. <u>And</u> she never questioned me charging her £4.50 for her windows, when everyone else only paid two quid! Well, she can afford it, can't she?

Max was another story. I knew from the off he'd be stuck up. Always keeping an eye on how well I was doing his windows, making sure he was getting his money's worth. It made overcharging him worthwhile.

founders of the Farnham dynasty.

Yes, there was Maxie boy, all big suit and cellphone. A right little poser. Made out he was dead upper class, from a rich background. Truth be known he started off as a working class lad from Blackburn.

So these two being nice, friendly neighbours was doomed from the start.

I suppose the first shot in the war was fired when Maxie finally had had enough of the Dixons' front garden looking like Steptoe's yard. But even worse! One of said items actually had the nerve to wander onto Maxie's property. Max went ballistic.

He saw his chance at revenge when he had a van from the council call to take away some old kitchen units from the Farnhams. The council worker asked Max if he wanted everything taken, and Max saw his chance at ridding the Close of the eyesore. So one bunged tenner later, and off went all of Ron's prize possessions to the local tip.

You should have seen old Dicko's face when he saw, or rather didn't see, all his gear.

Of course, he knew right away who was responsible. It was obvious. Plus the fact that I may have let slip to Ron that I saw who did it!

That's when Brookside's own Berlin Wall went up. The battle lines were drawn and God help anyone who tried to cross them. Unfortunately Ron's version was an odd combination of loads and loads of old doors, all colours and shapes, all nailed together and stretching all the way from the front to the back garden. It completely cut off communications between both households. In fact, the only way now for Max to have a go at Ron, was to knock on one of the doors and shout through the letter box!

Fortunately for everyone's sanity DD's brother Derek, a young, catholic priest, had got a bit friendly with the Farnhams' nanny - a lovely girl, loads of red hair, name of Margaret.

Well, these two got together and decided enough's enough. One night they pulled the whole lot down secretly, leaving Max with the impression that Ron had backed down, and vice versa. Stalemate.

Pulling the wall down wasn't the only development for Father Degsy and young Margaret. Some months later the latest scandal broke. I must admit to being a little more than gobsmacked to discover that our own version of the Thornbirds had been going on under our very noses! Next thing, Derek and Margaret are planning to run off together and he gets booted out of the church. Last I heard they were doing voluntary work together out in Bosnia. I hope they're still together - nice couple.

They'll never agree. They're arguing from different premises. →

Derek loved Margaret more than the Holy Church and their affair caused an unholy row.

Anyway the truce over the feud didn't last and Max still had plenty to keep his ulcer popping away. Young Tony Dixon, encouraged by his dad, Ron, no doubt, was up to all sorts, sneaking through the Farnhams' back garden with his scally mates. Setting Maxie's alarm off, knock and run, that sort of thing. One time, they removed every screw from the Farnhams' garden shed, and the whole lot collapses in a heap around him. There's Max, standing there, just holding the door handle.

It was tragic what happened to poor Tony. Killed in a big car smash. Ron's never got over it. Neither has Jimmy, cause it was his fault. Jimmy was just starting out on his rocky road to self destruction, and just got himself hooked on the stupid drugs. I don't know what he was playing at – I mean you hear of kids getting into drugs, and that's stupid enough. But Jimmy? He'd just turned forty and should have known better. But for some reason he gets hooked on that rubbish. He was out of his mind that day, his car caused the other car to swerve into a brick wall. Two lives wasted. Frank Rogers on his way to his wedding, along with young Tony Dixon. Both wiped out by that divvy Jimmy.

Of course the guilt and recriminations soon sobered him up. He even eventually got off the drugs. But now he thinks he's Mr Big. But I know he's now worse than the drug takers. He's a drug dealer. Pushing his ~~evol~~ evil wares onto poor unsuspecting kids.

I don't know why I've associated myself for so long with Jimmy. Maybe I believe one day he'll finally get his act together – some hope!

Ron still hates Jimmy, and who can blame him? Even Maxie's feud took a bit of a ~~hyatus~~ hiatus during that time. But it didn't last, of course.

Things were apparently a bit rocky between Ron and DD for some time. I suppose the death of Tony was the final straw, and they split up. But then Ron thought his life was just about to take a turn for the better, when in walked a young girl who immediately struck a chord with old Dicko. Well, it turned out to be more than a chord – more a complete overture. His and her eyes met across a large sliced, and two packets of luncheon meat. Ron's jaw hit the ground. This

Bev's hobby is Someone else's hobby.

was the girl who was going to completely change his life, this was Beverley McLoughlin, 21 years old, confident and trouble. Married men were her hobby.

So I suppose none of us should have been surprised when we heard DD had had a breakdown and gone off to some nunnery and Ron moved the new love of his life into Number 8.

Max and Patricia saw this as "Dixons Two – The Final Conflict". I think Max and Pat would have been happy to settle for Ron's old rubbish out on the lawn, or even Ron's very tasteful statuette in his back garden ornamental pond. Bev had big ideas to make sure she left her mark on the house – and what a mark! In came the four poster bed, along with the white plastic lampstand in the front garden. And her pièce de resistance? A sign over the door naming the place well and truly hers and Ron's! "Casa BevRon".

I'm surprised Max and Pat weren't putting up the For Sale sign outside their house, and emigrating to the back of beyond. But no, they stuck it out for some reason. I have a theory that Max actually <u>enjoys</u> his feud with Ron – I mean, it's probably more fun than squash.

But then there were the patter of tiny feet, and I don't mean Ron and Bev's little baby boy, Josh. No, this new arrival would really put the icing on the cake for relations between our two heroes.

This new tenant's name was Kiev. Kiev the chicken. Bev, who by now was the Farnhams' cleaner, was so impressed by Patricia's thoughts on good eating and sensible diets, thought she'd have a go herself and make Casa BevRon a veggie zone. Kiev was the master plan, who'd supply them with fresh, healthy, free range eggs. Ron pointed out a tiny flaw in her plan. Kiev was a he, not a she .... so unless any miracles were due to take place, the Dixons would be remaining an egg free household.

On top of all this, Max was no time pointing out the health hazards, not to mention the noise pollution, of having Kiev as a next door neighbour.

Although, for once, Ron had the same opinion on Kiev as Max, Ron saw this as a perfect opportunity to wind up his old sparring partner. Quick as a flash Ron jumped to Kiev's defence, and told Max to do one. Kiev would be staying, he'd always wanted a pet. Max crowed (3 times I think) but it was no good.

So while Max mustered the might of the residents' association, Bev thought she'd right her wrong by finding a chicken who would successfully supply them with eggs.
   Ron's heart deffo missed a beat as he walked into his kitchen that night, to be greeted by five, yes five, of Kiev's mates. She'd named then already; Butty, Tikka, Salad, Chasseur, and Soup.

Of course, Ron wasn't the only one to overact, Max did his bit as well. He went into orbit over this one.

Ron, me and a young bird. fowl play is not suspected.

Ron at the end of his tether!

But then each of the chickens started to go missing, one by one, under mysterious circumstances. No one quite knows where they went. Maybe they couldn't stand the constant arguing between Ron and Max. Maybe they ran away to join a circus. Who knows? But me and Ron have our own theories. Ron obviously thinks it was Maxie. Well, he does own a restaurant, doesn't he, so it would make sense.

But me, I'd blame Jimmy's dog Cracker – he's been looking a bit plump these days. And so the feud continues, and probably always will. The latest was when Max was talked into doing a bungee jump for charity. It was obvious from day one he didn't want to do it. He hasn't got a head for lows, never mind heights. But then Ron heard, and not to be outdone, decided, if it's good enough for Maxie ....

And so there's the two of them, scared witless, not wanting to be there, but both tied together, 150 feet in the air, about to plunge into oblivion on the end of a rubber band. Each of them was full of bravado, waiting for the other to back down.

At the last minute, just as the crowd were counting down, Max's bottle went. He couldn't do it. It was now left to Ron. No way could <u>he</u> back down. And so, Geronimoooooooo .... and Ron did it, he actually did it. He bounced around like a yo-yo.

Of course, we still hear non-stop of Ron's "death defying leap". In fact, he's still wearing his "bungee jumpers do it upside down" t-shirt. Much to Max's disgust, and shame.

Although the smile was wiped off Ron's face some time later, when he had a heart attack. All his gallivanting around, trying to keep up with the youthful Bev finally paid off and put an end to activities. From now on the most exciting thing for Ron to get heated up by was the lottery results. And even that wasn't to come his way. His next door neighbours, the Banks', scored on that one.

Still, I'm sure the quiet life won't suit Ron for long. Besides, Max misses him too much, and I'm sure the pair are plotting their next bout – seconds out, round three, ding, ding!

Me; Marcia + me Mum

Marcia Barrett was a wonderful girl who helped me find true happiness for a time – she was me first what you might call really serious relationship. She also helped me find me Mum.

I met Marcia through me mate, Mick Johno. She was his ex-wife Josie's bessy mate. Marcia was a real good laugh, dead easy going, just like me. We had loads in common, so it wasn't long before we had our first snog. The only thing that came between us back then was me stomach – maybe that's why girls find it difficult to get close to me.

With Marcia I found love. And me Mum.

CERTIFICATE OF BIRTH

No.	When and where born.	Name, if any.	Sex.	Name, and surname of father.	Name, surname, and maiden surname of mother.	Occupation of father.	Signature, description, and residence of informant.	When registered.	Signature of registrar.	Name entered after registration.
241	Twenty Sixth January 1957	Thomas Henry Edward	Boy	Sweeney Harold Sydney	Olive Norah. Mother.	Fitter	41 Geraghty Street Mother	Fifteenth February 1957	Ruby Combs	

Ruby E. Combs.
Registrar of Births and Deaths

Everyone knows now I was brought up in a children's home and never knew me parents.

One day, a couple of months after we decided we were serious about each other, Marcia said we ought to go on holiday, somewhere warm like Spain maybe. I said I didn't have a passport. Till then I'd taken the view that the less I existed in public documents — like Poll Tax lists and income tax forms — the better.

But I said I wouldn't mind going to Spain if I could go topless and she said legless, more like. Anyway, so I could get a passport she made me look out me birth certificate, which they'd given me when I left the home. I kept it in an old tin box.

Marcia was very keen to get a squint at it but I wouldn't let her. Kept asking me real name, because she'd only ever called me Sinbad.

So I said Sweeney and then she wanted to know the first names. I told her it just said Mr Sweeney. I don't know why I didn't want her to know the first-name column said Thomas Henry Edward. Bit embarrassed, I suppose. No ones called me Thomas or Tommy for years — since I was a kid.

Anyway the next thing Marcia starts getting carried away — fascinated about finding me roots and tracing the family tree. I told her they'd probably chopped it down years ago and built a supermarket over it.

But Marcia was a determined girl. That's why I liked her. She refused to give up.

I couldn't stop her after that. We had to find me parents, or at least discover what had happened to them. I'd spent half me life trying not to think about them. After all, they'd given me away when I was a baby, so they must be cruel people, mustn't they? That's how I saw it. Tell the truth, I was afraid <u>of finding out.</u>

But there was no holding Marcia. We had to go to the address on the birth certificate and after a bit of toing and froing we discovered the Mrs Sweeney who had lived there had died.

Next stop was the cemetery and Marcia found the grave. I was gutted, couldn't look at the inscription. Marcia was surprised I could be so emotional, but she was great. Hugged me till I felt better. Eventually I did have a look at the carved letters.

This is what it said: "Beloved husband. Harold Sydney Sweeney, died 1978, aged 71, Resting Where No Shadows Fall. Devoted mother. Olive Norah Sweeney, died 1981 aged 70, I Know That My Redeemer Liveth."

I was choked by the words "devoted mother." She hadn't been a devoted mother to me. She'd given me away. It was Marcia who made me see I wasn't Olive Sweeney's only child. There must have been other children. Me brothers or sisters. Me head was totally cabbaged by now.

Anyway I laid a bunch of flowers on the grave and we went.

I'd have let it lie there with me parents under that headstone. I didn't want to know any more. But Marcia was like a terrier with a bone. Or Cracker with Jimmy's ankle.

She couldn't let it go. Somehow she found out there was a Ruth Sweeney living in Runcorn in Cheshire and she worked out Ruth must be my sister. We went to the address and some middle aged woman with a small dog told us she knew nothing about it.

That should have been that. But Marcia was just as much a terrier as the woman's dog and she went back. Got past the front door and got the whole story. Talk about Inspector Morse.

Or what seemed like the whole story at that time. The woman admitted that she was Ruth Sweeney and that she was in fact my sister.

But her mother had had an affair with another bloke and I was his son, not her husband's. So they put baby Sinbad in the home, to hush it up like.

But Marcia didn't tell me this. Wasn't sure how I'd take it. She was waiting for the best time to let me in on the secret.

Enter Ellis Johnson. Ellis is the brother of Mick Johnson and if Mick is the nicest guy in the world, Ellis is the nastiest. You wouldn't credit two chalk-and-cheesers like that could exist in one family.

The thing is, Ellis and my Marcia used to be a couple. A long time before this, but they had been itemised.

Ellis was jealous that she now preferred me to a big, strong, handsome feller like himself.

He tells Marcia she was only going out with me through pity, because I'd got no-one, like. No family. She blurts out that I have got someone, a sister – even if I'm not entirely legitimate. And he cottons on that I don't know this yet.

Ellis being Ellis had to tell me, didn't he? Had to get in his little digs. More or less called me a bastard, an unwanted child, claimed Marcia really fancied him anyway.

I went for his throat. I surprised meself how brave I can get sometimes, for a devout coward. But the one I was really mad at was Marcia.

How could she? How could she tell Ellis and not tell me about Ruth? I had a right go at her and told her I never wanted to see her again.

But in the end we made up. I could never be angry at Marcia for long. She had such a nice, cheeky little face.

Anyway, I was all for going back to Ruth Sweeney. Marcia put me off, because Ruth had told her she couldn't bear to meet me.

In the end I just went. Ruth let me in, though she didn't want to. "You're me sister," I said. "We should have met years ago. We could have been a comfort to each other."

She thought about that. Then she said: "Deep down I really wanted you to find me."

We both felt a bit damp around the eyes, like.

Then she detonated the real bombshell.

"I lied to your friend Marcia," said Ruth.

"You mean you're not really me sister?"

"No," she said "I'm your mother."

To say I was double-gobsmacked would be the understatement of the century.

Marcia warned me not to expect too much from my "new" mother but in any case Ruth said she didn't want to see me again. I've felt rejected all me life but this last rejection was somehow the worst of all. I'd finally found me Mum and she just didn't want to know. Just as she didn't want to know way back in 1957 when she put me in the home.

Portrait of a young couple in love

Confusing when your sister turns out to be your Mum.

Marcia tried to comfort me but I wouldn't be comforted.

So Marcia went to see Ruth again and she showed her the little wristband from when I was born. That thing they put on babies so they don't get mixed up with the other babies.

Ruth had kept it all those years.

Couple of days later Ruth turns up on me doorstep and I get the whole story. How it happened. How I happened.

She was 17, innocent, ignorant, the way young girls were supposed to be in those days.

She'd gone on the bus with her mate Kath to a fairground at Blackpool. On the Waltzer they'd copped off with two lads. Ruth had arranged to meet hers later, one thing led to another and hows-yer-father – hows-my-father in fact – she was pregnant. Didn't even know the lad's right name, she just knew him as Figgy and she never saw him again. All she knew was she was terrified young Sinbad was on the way.

Her God-fearing parents were horrified, of course. The God-fearing always are. Ruth was packaged off to a relatives to hide the bump. I was somehow passed off as a late child of me grandmother and put into that home before you could say what-will-the-neighbours-think.

Ruth was in a right state after telling me all this and so was I. But in a way she was glad to get rid of that load of shame she'd carried all those years by talking about it.

Afterwards I felt wonderful, though. Sort of elated. I knew me Mum hadn't really ditched me because she didn't love me. She was a frightened teenager forced into it. Suddenly I really existed. I was part of a family. I felt so good I decided to ask Marcia to marry me. I wish I could say the course of true love ran smooth, but it ran more like Zig Zag Street, where the old Liverpool MP Bessie Braddock lived.

I went to see Ruth who said she was glad Marcia and I were getting hitched but she couldn't possibly come to the wedding. In spite of everything she still couldn't acknowledge me in public. Not at that

Marcia's answer to my proposal lit up the scoreboard - and my life.

stage. Too much water under Runcorn Bridge and all that.

But she did give me that baby wristband. It was the nearest thing I had to a family tree.

True to form, Ellis kept causing trouble, it's a chronic condition with him, but I managed to choose a ring for Marcia and things looked okay for a bit.

But, as they say the path of true love walks a wonky path and Marcia was starting to get cold feet about setting a wedding date. In the end she confessed she couldn't have kids, because of some infection she'd had in the past.

I assumed Ellis gave it to her. Wrongly as it happened but I went for him. Let me emotions get carried away again. Told Marcia we could always adopt, I still wanted her.

But she disappeared, leaving her engagement ring behind. Too many harsh words had been spoken. She returned for a time — we had a tearful reunion on a coach coming back from an outing to Alton Towers — but me and Marcia was never meant to be. We tried, but it just wasn't the same.

In the end we fell out when I discovered she was helping Josie, Mick Johnson's wife, to sneak his kids away from him.

Josie was the wife-from-Hell and Johno was one of me bezzy mates, so I wasn't having that. Gave Marcia a right earful for being a party to it.

Marcia told me to get lost but then a few days later changed her mind and wanted to forgive me.

I hadn't changed mine and wasn't about to forgive her. Wanted to, but I just couldn't.

Sad end of romance, with Marcia disappearing finally into the sunset. Just like in the pictures. But this time I was left watching the credits on me own.

I thought me heart was broken but it wasn't permanent. It wasn't long after that Mandy Jordache came into my life.

I went to see me Mum again, at the library where she worked. But she'd gone. Probably couldn't take the shock of suddenly meeting her handsome young son ....

I knew the score and understood. But then, some time later, after I'd met Mandy, me Mum got in touch again. Out of the blue, just like that, as Tommy Cooper once said.

She'd not been too well, and she'd let her home fall into disrepair. To be honest, when me and Mandy went round there, no way could I have left her living in that place alone.

It was Mandy's idea to bring her back to the Close. Actually she settled in okay, while I worked at getting her own house ship shape.

I felt great having me Mum living with us again. And it led to me finding out about me Uncle Jake.

I had even _more_ relatives than ever now. Me Mum's brother, Jake, moved out to Australia years ago .... but he'd kept in touch with Mum on and off.

This latest letter contained an offer no one could refuse. He only wanted her to go out to the land of Rolf Harris and stay with them! And the invite extended to me.

Of course I considered it. Who wouldn't? But at that time I was waiting on Mandy finally declaring her true feelings for

At first me Mum wouldn't let me into her life— or even her house

me, so in the end decided to put away me bilabong and me digareedoo. And so I waved goodbye to me Mum once more. I get some cracker letters and photies from her. Sitting in the sun with me relatives — cousins, aunties, the lot. A Sweeney in every port of the world!

But I got one letter, out of the blue, that worried me. Looked very official, from a solicitors. Telling me to come along to "discuss me Mum's estate". Estate? She didn't even have a van.

I took Jimmy along with me for support. I was convinced I was gonna get bad news about me poor old mum.

When I came out the solicitors I was in shock, deep shock. Jimmy put his arm around me in sympathy "never mind mate, you'll get over it."

Bit this is a surprise I deffo would <u>never</u> get over. Me Mum hadn't passed away. On the contrary, she was healthier than ever.

She'd decided to live out the rest of her days in kangaroo country. And as she no longer had a use for her house, had sold it .... and given <u>me</u> the full proceeds — £45,000!

I was rich.

Me and Jimmy danced around, hardly believing it.

I knew straight off what I wanted to spend it on. Mandy was worried as the charity were selling her house, so I bought it — lock, stock and patio.

Of course, sometime later, Jimmy bought it off me, so now I'm going round with forty-five grand burning a hole in me keck's pocket.

I don't know what I'll spend it on — maybe I'll get the old cork hat out and pay a visit to me mum. You never know, I might emigrate.

But on second thoughts maybe not. How could I let me regular customers down? Besides, I'm on a diet and not really into barbies (bbq's not the doll's!)

MICK AND MARIANNE

Jimmy Corkhill's been me bezzy mate for years but since he took to dealing smack I've had to relegate him.

I suppose the bezzy mate title now goes to Mick Johno, well Johnson as he appears on the voting register.

Mick's the best guy in the world and he's had the worst luck. Particularly with women. Most recently with a nutty schoolteacher called Jenny who thought he was madly in love with her. Mick didn't want to know, but she made a kind of shrine to him in her room – like a holy place in which she kept umpteen pictures of Mick and old pairs of his socks she'd nicked. Now that is obsession. I've smelt his socks.

Really scarey, that was. Got Mick into all kinds of bother. (The girl – not the socks.) Thank God I was able to help him through some of it.

But women have spelled trouble in Mick's life since puberty, I guess. He had a terrible time with his wife Josie, a fiery girl from Wales who came in and out of his life like a yo-yo, spending all his money, leaving him in dire debt, even kidnapping his kids Leo and Gemma once

The only good thing I can say about Josie was that she introduced me to her mate Marcia, who was the love of my young life for quite some time.

What I really want to tell you about is Mick and a pretty nice woman called Marianne Dwyer. I mean she was pretty and *nice*.

I really thought he'd found the old life partner in her and so did Mick.

When Mick first appeared in the Close he was a driver for a funeral firm. But it

Me, Mick + a merry-go-round, a sort of symbol of his love life.

was a dead end job and he became a taxi driver. He lodged with Harry Cross in the bungalow at Number 6 and when Mick said he'd like to have his kids stay over sometimes – he was living apart from Josie who'd gone off with her fancy man, Tony – big-hearted Harry said why not? But he'd have to put the rent up a few bob. All heart was Harry.

Mick first met Marianne when he was staging a protest about the closing down of a local school. She was working for the education authority and he fancied her straight away. I think he fancied a spot of detention.

But Josie came back on one of her yo-yo visits and Marianne took up with Mick's brother Ellis, an operator so smooth he'd make Hugh Grant look tongue-tied.

Well, Marianne was taken in by flash man – just as my Marcia was for a time – and Mick had his hands full with Josie the spendthrift, who brought him pretty well to bankruptcy before she finally hit the trail with her Tony.

He was buying the bungalow by then but he was getting hassled for back payments so he told the building society to stick their mortgage in their repossession file and moved into the flat over the Pizza Parlour in Brookside Parade.

By then he'd given up the cabbying and was devoting his life to Italian cheese on toast

Ellis and Marianne got engaged, though Mick told me he was head-over-trainers with the girl himself. But being the shy guy he is he couldn't tell her. The couple got right to the altar before Marianne dashed out, leaving Ellis with his mean mouth gaping open. I had a little holiday in me heart over that, I must admit.

Marianne realised it was Mick she really loved, but that was just the start of a long line of troubles. He gave her a ring but she said it was too soon after Ellis to get engaged, so she agreed to wear it on her right hand.

Then Marianne lost her job. Mick was all for her helping out at the Pizza Parlour but Marianne was a bit middle-class for that. She reluctantly did a few shifts but then got herself a big-paying job with a firm called Grearsons.

Her boss was a right slimeball called Charles Weekes. Nobody ever called him Charlie, though that's what he was. A right one. Well this Charlie was split from his wife and his one ambition was to replace her with Marianne. Maybe he should have formed a club with Ellis.

Charlie took her away on some course and joined her in the jacuzzi. Uninvited, like. Spotted her birthmark. Mick got jealous, obviously and had a couple of really bad rows with Marianne. She didn't want to give up her new career but she was getting so much trouble from Charles that she thought she might have to.

One time he even stole a pair of her knickers – she wasn't wearing them at the time – and said he'd keep them as a souvenir. But I don't think they were his size.

Eventually she threatened to do him for sexual harassment with the company management and Charles turned nasty. Nastier, I should say.

Tells Mick he's been having an affair with Marianne and Mick, soft as he is, believes him when he describes her birthmark and her knickers. Suggests Mick talks her out of the sexual harassment thing.

Mick believed him and was gutted.

But eventually Marianne made Mick see the truth, though she lost her case with the management. So she took it up with the Equal Opportunities Commission.

Charles tried bribery this time. A great new job with more money if she'd only say she imagined him putting the hard word on her. Mick being Mick he lost his temper and decked Charles. Put him right on his back. The bizzies thought there was nothing in it when Charles complained, but then he threatened a private prosecution against Mick for assault.

Though he'd forget it if Marianne dropped her charges against him. In the end she did but trapped Charles finally by secretly tape-recording him saying how much he fancied her and how he'd make her a star if she said yes.

Played the tape to the firm's management, leaving Charles looking like a postbox. Red with his mouth wide open. But that wasn't the end of Marianne's problems. Angry at her for exposing their Charles, the firm transferred her to Newport! She couldn't face the journey, only saw Mick and the kids at weekends and before long she resigned. Worked with Mick in the Pizza Parlour for a bit and then got herself a nice little number in personnel at a local place called Litrotech.

Steady Eddie Banks worked there and from the start there was a bit of friction between Marianne and Eddie. Well, a lot, actually.

There were big rumours about redundancy and Eddie wanted to know the truth. Marianne couldn't tell him, of course and there were all kinds of ructions. There was a strike, what the telly calls scenes of industrial unrest, with Marianne caught between her firm and her neighbour Eddie.

In the meantime Mick had got involved with coaching teenage kids at football. He's always been a great sportsman, has Mick, and coaching kids was close to his big heart.

There was this problem kid Garry from a one-parent family and Mick did his best for him. His Mum Carol took a shine to Mick and that caused a bit of trouble between Mick and Marianne. Well, a load of trouble, tell the truth. But Mick and Marianne finally got round to actually setting a wedding date and she moved Mick's ring from her right hand to third finger left.

I was made up for the both of them. After a lifetime of grief it looked as if Mick was finally going to settle down with the girl of his dreams. The girl of quite a lot of guys' dreams, now I come to think of it. I might have had the odd dream about her meself, except I was occupied with Marcia at the time.

There was only one thing left between them. Marianne wanted somewhere better to live than the over-the-shop flat.

First she found a big old house which she loved, but Mick wanted a modern place, like. Finally smooth Maxie Farnham – by this time wearing his estate agent's outfit – found them a new place, a showhouse that he could let them have very reasonably. (In other words he couldn't sell the property.)

Luckily they both liked it, made an offer, found a deposit and set about chasing a mortgage.

By this time Garry, the teenager from hell was staying with the Johnson family, kipping on the couch. Marianne wasn't best pleased. The place wasn't big enough for her and Mick, Leo and Gemma, as it was.

Mick saw Marianne first, Ellis got her, Mick got her back and she ended up on her own. I think they call it the infernal triangle.

And Garry wasn't exactly what you'd call the perfect houseguest. Especially when his dad Greg, more or less a professional criminal, came out of jail.

Naturally Mick helped him. Well, he would, wouldn't he? Help anybody-anytime-anywhere. That's my mate Johno.

Gave Greg work in the Pizza Parlour.

Greg repaid him by threatening to move into Mick's overstuffed flat and plotting a robbery at Marianne's firm.

By this time Marianne was beginning to come round to the workers' point of view in their dispute with the staff-cutting management, which caused the bizzies to get suspicious later on.

Anyway Greg boasted to Jimmy Corkhill that he'd be set up for life after this monster job he was going to pull. The robbery happened and Greg got away with just two hundred quid.

Hardly enough to set him up for the weekend. Eddie Banks got a look at the disguised robber and got the idea it was Mick.

Put him in a very difficult position.

Of course Mick didn't know anything about all this when his wedding day dawned.

Turned up to marry his Marianne but the bizzies declared a just impediment.

They were there to nick both Mick and Marianne for armed robbery. Greg had exchanged his stolen £200 for notes in the Pizza Parlour till. The bizzies found them and elected Mick the armed robber. Helped by his girlfriend who happened to work for Litrotech and wasn't too happy about the way they did business. In the end they didn't charge Marianne with anything, but they did Mick all right. He got out on police bail and looked forward to a trial and possibly imprisonment. But when he

Togetherness for the two Ms, but it didn't last.

Mick was left alone with the kids again. Story of his life.

a trial and possibly imprisonment. But when he asked Marianne if she'd look after his kids, should he be sent away, he got the wrong answer.

Marianne thought the kids should go to their mother, if the worst came to the worst. Mick was <u>dead</u> against this. So they fell out again. He said love me, love my kids.

She took off for the new house, leaving Mick in the flat. Said a few days apart would help them work things out. What's more she'd been offered a big job in Glasgow.

Like a fool Mick forbids her to take it and Marianne doesn't take too kindly to that word.

Anyway Garry finally did the right thing and grassed on his Dad. Mick shook the truth out of Greg, the law was informed and Mick Johno was finally a free man.

His name was cleared so he should have gone ahead and wed Marianne.

But all the troubles and tensions had been too much for the couple. Marianne handed Mick the keys to the new house, wished him a merry Christmas and said she'd be moving to Glasgow as from January 1.

Leaving Mick to enjoy a very happy New Year.

I hope Mick meets the real right girl some day. In fact, I'd marry him meself, if it'd make him happy. Only joking, like .... not my type. Too tall. Maybe me and him could cop off with a pair of sisters .... have a double wedding. That way I'd get a wife <u>and</u> keep me bezzy mate.

THE JORDACHE STORY

I first met Mandy Jordache the way I met most people in Brookside, by cleaning her windows. I'd heard on the Close telegraph that Mandy and her daughters Beth and Rachel had been put into the empty Number 10 by some charity. She'd been a battered wife and Number 10 was a safe house - safe from her brute of a husband Trevor. Or so Many thought at the time. It was supposed to be some big secret, but that's impossible on Brookside Close.

We became friends, and I helped out when I could. She had the usual troubles with the girls, Rachel at school, clever Beth at college studying to be a doctor. Mandy was upset when it turned out Beth was more interested in girls then blokes, though I knew about that before her mother did. (I caught her in a clinch with Margaret Clemence, the Farnham's nanny. Even I knew girls don't kiss each other like that.

What Beth felt for
Margaret was love.
And she dared
speak its name.

Trevor knocks at the door...

Not in a two-minute clinch. I pretended not to notice . . .)

Trouble was never far away from the door of Number 10 and one day Mandy's past caught up with her. Or rather her past husband caught up with her. Trevor Jordache, who'd gone to jail for battering Mandy, found out where she was living.

The finest butter from Kerry wouldn't melt in clever Trevor's mouth, you'd bet on that just from a glimpse of his smarmy smile.

The man was a nutter, a dangerous and violent nutter. He wanted to control Mandy and the girls completely and he wanted them to love him unconditionally while he was doing any perverted thing that came into his head. Although, of course, he'd changed, so he said, a reformed man - ha!!

I'm no Dr Freud, Dr Spock or Captain Kirk for that matter, so I can't tell you how the thought police would explain what was wrong

...and tragedy walks in

with Trevor's head. But whatever it was he wanted locking up for good. And the key thrown in the Mersey.

God knows how but Mandy somehow let him back into her home, into her life. Even though he'd raped Beth, his own daughter. He raped Mandy too, and beat her.

No-one knew this, of course. It all went on behind the closed doors of Number 10. If I'd known I'd have killed him, peaceable bloke though I am.

Mandy and Beth managed to keep the truth from Rachel, Mandy's younger daughter, who thought the sun shone out of Trevor's armpit.

But it was when Trevor started his perverted, child-molesting tricks on Rachel that Mandy and Beth went over the edge, and who can blame them?

They decided to kill Trevor, destroy the madman with weedkiller and painkillers in his whisky. Didn't work, so maybe they should have used rat poison. Though you'd need a lot of poison to kill that big rat. Trevor just went into a violent rage. He attacked Beth, shouting that he'd kill them all, including himself.

No-one deserves
to go through
what my
Mandy did.

Desperate days. None of us knew what to do.

Mandy picked up a kitchen knife to save her daughter and stabbed Trevor in the back without thinking - she just did it. What else could she do?

This is about the time I turned into Columbo (without the dirty mac). I found the knife, I saw the pile of earth out the back garden, I listened when Rachel complained her father wasn't around and I put two and two together. Who says I'm not smart at arithmetic?

I worked out that Trevor hadn't gone far. He was lying low just a few yards from Mandy's back door, in fact. I didn't tell Mandy I knew. I can't tell you how I felt when I realised what had gone on. Gutted that this excuse for a human being had driven Mandy to murder. No, I won't say murder. If ever there was such a thing as justifiable homicide this was it. Trevor Jordache didn't deserve to take another breath. In fact I wished it was me who'd killed him.

So I offered to build Mandy a patio in her back garden. She said she'd be grateful - and I knew that she would be grateful for more than having a few tasteful paving stones to sunbathe on. I knew and she knew - but neither of us put into words - that the patio was Trevor's headstone.

And so that was where he stayed. For almost two years. Mandy and me had our ups and down, but throughout this time we grew closer. I was falling in love, I don't mind telling you, and I hoped that Mandy felt the same way about me - I think she did, but after all that had gone on, who could blame her?

January, 1995, and I decided that what me and Mandy needed was a holiday, away from the back garden lodger. I took Mandy and Rachel over to Ireland, just outside of Dublin for a winter break. Beth stayed behind to have the house, and her latest girlfriend, to herself.

But of course, clever Trevor was getting bored and wanted to make a reappearance, didn't he?

What brought him back was a flood in next door's garden. The Bankses, who live there, first noticed a puddle, then it turned into a lake. They poked around and decided that the water was coming from our garden. From under my patio, in fact.

Steady Eddie Banks (who's got the idea I'd buried something valuable under the patio and who had a wife, kids and Harley Davison to support) decided to start lifting out patio flags to find the source of the leak. Than Beth came home. Shaking like a ton of jelly Beth ordered him off before they came across the patio foundation - the body of Trevor Jordache.

When Mandy and I got back home we were feeling pretty good, thinking just maybe we could be permanently together. Till Beth spoke up about the Bankses raiding the patio.

Mandy said we'd have to move the body - when Rachel was out of the way, of course. But when it came to it she just couldn't do it. Beth, who seemed to be thinking for all of us, said we'd just have to run.

The Water Board sent a mechanical digger to find the source of Lake Banks and Mandy and I knew it wouldn't be long before they moved into our garden.

We collected Rachel from school, told her some cock and bull story. Then Mandy, Rachel, Beth and me made for the ferry back to Ireland.

We put up in a bed and breakfast and looked at the papers next morning with a feeling of terror. Nothing about a body turning up in a Liverpool suburb. I suppose we were relived but in a funny way I was sorry the body hadn't been reported. Back of my mind I knew we couldn't run forever.

Rachel didn't know what was going on and kept asking to go home from this extended holiday.

I shared a room with Mandy but slept on the chair.

I found out later what was going on at Number Ten. The digger had moved most of the patio and Eddie Banks jumped into the hole. Discovered a plastic bag, ripped it open expecting to find my "treasure" and shook hands with Trevor - I must admit I'd like to have seen his face.

Trevor had fingered us from beyond the grave. The bizzies came, of course, the area was sealed off, the Close went mad with excitement. As Bing would say, "The balloon's gone up!"

Mandy said we must have been crazy to think we'd get away with murder. Next morning she went out and just for a time I thought she'd done something silly. But she came back with the papers. They ruled our lives in those days, the papers.

A happy holiday snap from Ireland.

In the end there was an item in an Irish paper. A very small item about a body being unearthed in a Liverpool back yard. That was it. The game was up.

We felt we had to tell Rachel the truth and what a mistake that was. She took off from that little B and B like a rocket and disappeared from sight the way a rocket does.

We wandered the streets looking for her, eventually spotted her in a police car. We went to the police station, unsure what Rachel had said to the Garda, and nervously asked for her back.

They said okay but fill in these forms, so we grabbed Rachel and ran. We weren't about to fill in any forms.

Took a bus to Dublin without getting caught. Next morning's papers told us the body had been identified as Trevor's and that the bizzies knew we were in Ireland.

I knew how a fish in a net feels as it's being dragged in. Rachel saw Trevor's photo in the paper and broke down. I think we all felt like throwing ourselves in the River Liffey that morning.

We booked into another B and B but the girl on the desk must have been on Mastermind, got suspicious and called the local law. We found somewhere else but we knew we had to keep moving.

We decided to move down the coast, though we all knew it couldn't be long before they caught us. But in that terrible atmosphere of strain and fear Mandy and I went to bed together for the first time.

I couldn't believe anyone could feel happy on the run from the police but I was. So was Mandy. We were made up. We felt sort of . . . married.

We had supper that night in some big pub - the last supper I saw it as later - and there was a Garda in there, a big Irish bizzie. He left and we felt safe, but we never were anything like safe.

As we left the pub it was like a scene from a Hollywood cop film. Squad cars screaming up, enough police to quell a football riot and we were well and truly nicked.

SINBAD QC

When we were brought back from Ireland by the bizzies I tried to take all the blame, told them it was me who killed Trevor. But they weren't having any of it. In the end they charged Mandy with murder and her and Beth with conspiracy to murder. Rachel, of course, who'd known nothing about the whole business of Trevor's death, burial, disinterment, reburial and resurrection at the time, wasn't involved with the law. Jimmy says I was dead lucky not to be charged as an accessory - but I'd have changed places with Mandy no problem.

I was terrified they'd keep Mandy and Beth locked up but luckily they were remanded on bail so, we all went back to Number 10, which I'd managed to buy with some money me Mum gave me.

Rachel decided she couldn't live with the people who'd killed her Dad so David and Jean Crosbie took her in. Thank God for good neighbours.

We had a couple of months to ourselves. It was a funny time, I can tell you. Mandy and Beth were terrified of the coming trial, of course, and so was I, I don't mind telling you. To finally be together with Mandy but to know there was the chance of her being taken away from me. That was a kind of Hell. I proposed to her but she wasn't sure it was fair on me, marrying someone who could become a jailbird.

Then amongst all this grief, the best thing ever happened. Mandy discovered she was pregnant. I was totally gobsmacked and made up!!

You wouldn't credit it, but it happened that first time we did it in Dublin, when we were on the run. In a way I took it as a sign that everything was going to be okay. Having a kid with Mandy would be just about the best thing that every happened to me. Me, a Dad! Who'd have thought it, eh?

But of course, the happiness didn't last - the hate mail started coming. Terrible anonymous letters saying Mandy and Beth were evil women who would rot in Hell for what they did to Trevor.

Do you wonder we couldn't say cheese for the camera?

Bing + Jean tried to get Rachel to talk.

I'm telling you, they should have got medals for what they did.

Death threats even - one letter had a lethal dose of tablets. There's some sick minds out there.

Rachel wouldn't talk to her Mum, though the Crosbies tried to persuade her. Everybody was very good in the Close; they knew what Mandy had been through and their sympathy helped. But we couldn't help wondering if one of them was sending those disgusting letters.

I took Mandy out shopping for maternity clothes and we both enjoyed that, though she had a little weep when she looked at baby clothes. Must admit, got a bit emotional meself. Had trouble hiding the lump in me throat - we were both thinking about our child being born in prison.

I don't know how I felt when the trial began. Scared, of course, but protective to Mandy and Beth as much as I could have. Worried about what Rachel would say. She'd been called as a witness for the prosecution.

Put me bezzy suit on, shirt and tie, new pair of black shoes, looked like I was going to me wedding - if only. There was a wait for the judge - busy sitting in judgement on some other poor bugger apparently - so Mandy, Beth and me sat in the court tearoom. Our lady solicitor Alison, was cheerful. Said we had a good chance and our barrister, Mr Anderson, was one of the best. We needed all the help we could get.

A few of the neighbours turned up to sit in the public gallery. Mick Johno arrived with Bing, Ron Dixon with Bev although I think they only came for a nose. Bev started taking illegal pictures in the court with her little camera and had it confiscated in the courtroom. "Spoilsport!" she said. "We only want a few shapshots as a souvenir." What's she like, eh?

I suppose all the people from the Close had come out of curiosity, it's true, but also out of sympathy for us. Showing solidarity, like. But Beth saw them as vultures, really, come to pick her and Mandy's bones. She really had a go at them, told them to clear off. There

was me, looking like one of Harry Enfield's scousers "calm down! Calm down!"

She was in a funny state altogether. Frightened, naturally enough. I mean the age of her, having to cope with all this, most teenagers only have to worry about a few spots. But she was really off her head that she and her Mum were in the dock when the real criminal was Trevor Jordache. And he'd got what he deserved.

I showed Mandy the engagement ring I'd brought her and we both got a bit moist-eyed. Mandy went to the loo and was followed in by the wicked witch of the North West. Trevor's sister Brenna, who makes the bride of Frankenstein look like Bonnie Langford.

Brenna had a right go at Mandy, shouted and screamed that she'd rot in jail for killing her wonderful Trev. Mandy was too stunned to answer back, but some of Brenna's words and phrases were just the same as the ones in the anonymous letters. So at last we knew who'd been sending the hate mail. We should have realised.

Finally here comes the judge and the trial gets started. I was in a funny position. Because I

As Bev found out, you're not allowed to take photos in court, but a newspaper artist sketched Mandy & Beth in the dock.

was giving evidence for the defence I wasn't allowed in court, so I sat about in corridors and waiting rooms. I felt terrible, knowing that my Mandy was in there being legally gutted while I was just resting on my jacksie. I started pacing up and down, at least it was good practice for when Mandy went into labour.

I found out what was happening in the breaks - recesses they call them - through some of the others who had been in court. Some of it I read later in the Echo, because the case was attracting a lot of attention from the press and the telly. Funny, you always dream, when you're a kid of being famous. But I thought I'd end up on Top of the Pops, not Crimewatch.

It looked bad for Beth and Mandy when the prosecution opened their case. The prosecution barrister was a right nasty piece of work. I never really found out his name though we called him the Moustache, because he had a growth on his upper lip you'd need a hedgeclipper to trim. Big handlebar job. Made him look even more fierce, wonder if it was false?

If you listened to him you'd think Mandy and Beth were the most evil women since

Medusa. The trouble is the jury were listening to him, and believing every word.

He called Brenna - our barrister took the mick by privately naming that holier-than-everyone woman Mother Teresa - and in return she called Mandy every name in the universe. Apparently she called me "a bad smell" and Mandy's "fancy man". Obviously doesn't like me aftershave. Her beloved Trevor might have gone to jail for inflicting grievous bodily harm on Mandy but that was the only time he'd touched her and she'd driven him to it. Well, that was Brenna's story. Jackanory or what . . ?!

Trevor was this amazing saint who'd never laid a lecherous finger on the girls, Brenna the bitch told the court.

Poor Rachel was sad and confused in the witness box, they told me. Denied that her father had ever touched her, though she admitted he had got into bed with her to keep warm. She got so upset under cross-questioning that Mandy shouted from the dock to leave her alone, even though it was Rachel's evidence that was stitching her up. We were all relying on Rachel to admit that her father had interfered with her and that's why Mandy killed him.

Rachel did some more harm by saying Beth had it in for her father "because she hates all men." Alright, so what if Beth was gay? I must admit, I was a bit shocked meself when I first found out. But once I got used to it, I just thought live and let live. Not that I have those tendencies meself, you understand.

When it was our turn Mandy went into the box and was made into Robinson's mincemeat by the Moustache. She tried to tell the truth about what Trevor had done but the Moustache twisted everything she said. If Trevor had been battering her for 20 years and interfering with the girls why hadn't she gone to the police earlier, he sneered.

Mandy's answer - that she was scared - was true but didn't sound too good to the jury.

Rachel didn't tell the truth, the whole truth and nothing but the truth. Nothing like the truth, more like.

Then there was another break and batty Brenna cornered Mandy again in the loo. Maybe she had a toilet fixation. This time Mandy was ready for the twisted cow. Mandy told her she was glad she'd killed Trevor and she'd do it again. Then she gave Brenna a smack in the mouth. Yiss! Go on, girl, nice one! I'd have given anything to see that.

Beth was next in to bat. She didn't do herself much good giving evidence. She shouted out about the unfairness of it all and got warned by the judge for contempt of court. Talk about making things worse.

But she did make it clear she'd seen Trevor in bed with Rachel and how it brought back to her the horror of being raped by him, herself.

"This man," she shouted " was living with three women and he was raping them all! He deserved to die. He was a psychopath, an animal - and it's us who are on trial!"

Then it was my turn in the box. It's funny, but I'd run over and over in me mind what I was going to say. Some brilliant speech, that'd get the girls off. I wanted to find the words to tell them that Mandy had done no more than protect herself and her family.

But I'm not very good with words. And once I was up there, with all those faces looking at me . . . well lets just say I wish I'd worn brown kecks.

I had to tell everyone about my relationship with Mandy, how I'd known her for two years and fallen in love with her. It even had to come out how we'd first had sex in Ireland. Talk about personal! The Moustache had some fun with that. He made out Mandy and me were in some big plot to get rid of Trevor so we could be together.

I told the truth but it didn't seem to cut much ice.

Things looked a bit rough for Mandy and Beth, I had to admit that. But at least I was allowed to sit in court once I had given my evidence. At least I could see the woman I loved in the Dock, holding hands with her daughter for comfort.

We smiled at each other as best we could. It wasn't much but it was something.

Before we knew it, it was almost the final whistle. The Moustache was on his feet, making his closing speech, making the whole business sound like a right hammer horror story with Trevor the innocent victim and Mandy and Beth a pair of cold-blooded killers. And me the simple sap who got drawn in by an evil serial killer. It would have made me laugh if it wasn't making me cry.

But our man Mr Anderson was brill when he said his final words. He talked about the ordeal the Jordache women went through for years "not knowing if Trevor Jordache would kiss them or punch them." You could have heard a pin drop.

He looked straight at the jury when he said: "They couldn't run, they couldn't hide, what else could they do to stop him? If you find them guilty you will be sweeping the issue of domestic violence under the carpet."

Then the judge summed up. He seemed a decent feller, under his wig, fair-minded like. It sounded like he was telling the jury to bring in a manslaughter verdict and I felt a bit more cheerful.

Next day I took Beth and Mandy back to court in a taxi for the verdict. We didn't know if they'd walk free or rot in jail the way Brenna wanted. We didn't know what to say to each other, so we sat in silence. When we got to court there was a crowd of women demonstrating, waving placards, so we had to force our way in.

I found out later they were on Mandy's side, speaking up against rape and wife battering, but at the time they just seemed to get in the way.

The jury were still deliberating, so we sat in the tearoom. I tried to guess what was going on in the jury room. I didn't like the look of the foreman, a big bald bloke in a yellow sweater and glasses. I just had this idea he was against us. I think I've always judged people by their appearance - this time I hoped to God I was wrong.

Jimmy Corkhill came in and I knew he was after something. You can't know Jimmy for ten years and more and not know when he had a scam going. He started saying I wouldn't want to rattle about in that big house on me own - Number Ten has four bedrooms - if, you know, the worst happened. He meant if Mandy and Beth went down.

He thought it wouldn't be a bad idea if he and his Jackie moved in, just to keep me company like. I couldn't believe even Jimmy would try that at such a time. I wanted to smack him one but I thought it would make things worse. I just said: "What did you get when they were giving out hearts?"

Didn't make any difference to Jim, who could teach a rhinoceros how to grow thicker skin. I suppose deep down Jimmy's alright. Always been a bit of a scally . . . but now he's into all this stupid drug dealing lark, I can't call him a mate any more.

Big Bad Brenna confronted us in the corridor. She had Rachel with her and she played her rot-in-jail record again to Beth and Mandy. Hit Mandy with a bombshell when she said Rachel was going to live with her in Ireland.

But Mandy told Rachel about Brenna's hate mail and you could see Rachel believed it. She finally said she'd sooner go on staying with the Crosbies.

Mandy and I had a short time alone before the jury came back. Long enough for me to give her the ring I'd bought and tell her I'd love her forever.

"I've ruined your life," she said.

I squeezed her hand and told her: "You talk more rubbish than anyone else I know." I put the ring on her finger and said "With this ring I thee . . ." but I couldn't finish. Too choked, just too choked.

Someone said the jury were coming back but we couldn't find Beth. She'd locked herself in the loo, trembling with fear. Eventually the solicitor talked her out and hugged her. "I don't want to go to prison," Beth sobbed. Suddenly this outspoken spirited young woman became a little girl again.

I still dream about that verdict. The foreman said they found Mandy guilty of murder and conspiracy to murder and Beth guilty of conspiracy. Brenna smiled, I remember that.

And then the judge passed sentence. He

reckoned he was sorry and all that, but the law said he couldn't do anything else but sentence Mandy to life imprisonment. Beth was given five years . . .Life . . .? But that's forever . . .!

I found meself diving up and shouting "You can't do that! Are you deaf or something? Didn't you hear what she went through?"

They tried to stop me but I forced my way to the dock and kissed Mandy goodbye.

"I'll wear the ring, I'll never take it off," she said.

Then they took her and her daughter down the steps! I don't think I've ever felt pain like that, and I hope I never do again, as long as I live.

Next day it was all systems go . . . I suppose I could have just sat around, feeling sorry for meself, but this needed action, so I called round the troops. Well, not exactly an army, but Bing's residents association - BRA . . . well, what better place to go for support?

The 'Free The Brookside Two' campaign was up and running, with plenty of help from the residents and some womens' groups.

We did the lot. Posters, T-shirts, leaflets, anything to make sure everyone knew about this massive injustice. Alison, the girls' solicitor said she'd put in for an appeal, but as much attention as possible would help. I must admit, I really threw meself into it and it helped take me mind

Brookside rallied round to get the gurls out.

Jean rather enjoyed being a rebel.

off things. Nearly ended up in nick meself though, when me and little old Jean Crosbie got nabbed by the bizzies, as we were sticking up a load of campaign posters. I was mortified. But I'm sure I saw a satisfied grin on Jean's face. I think she actually enjoyed being a "fugitive from the law", as she saw it. Luckily, the bobbies who picked us up just gave us a bit of a slapped wrist. They were alright really, and as we were let go, one of them winked and said "Good luck with the campaign!" They knew the score.

All that week I had to keep calming Jean down, who now had the taste for adventure and a life of crime. I don't know what got into her . . . she kept going on saying she wanted to join one of these Lesbian activist thingy groups "Sisters are doing it to themselves" she kept saying was her new motto. And of course, her hubby, Bing, kept blaming me for leading her on. I mean, what do I know about lesbians? For that matter, what does Jean . . .?

So the campaign hotted up. We even had a big candle-lit vigil on the steps of St. Georges' Hall. It was supposed to be women only, but this was about my Mandy, so me and Mick Johno gatecrashed. I felt dead funny though being the only fellas. All those women, and no dance floor . . . I told Mick he should use this opportunity to cop off, but he wasn't having any - said he was too shy!

All this time I was visiting the girls in the prison as much as I could. God, what a wrench having to leave Mandy and my unborn child behind, when I had to go home. I always tried me best to keep up the old stiff lip, and put on a brave face for the girls. But inside, I was tearing apart.

It did them a bit of good hearing of all the campaign events we'd organised. I told them about Rosie Banks putting together a marathon darts match. Even though Rosie was pregnant! Her husband, Eddie, wasn't best pleased to see his expectant wife up all night and eventually she was confined to barracks. But Rosie felt she wanted to stay involved, and after a while she went awol. We'd organised our best stunt ever. We were going to stay outside the prison - a peaceful protest - until the girls were released.

Every day and night kipping there, the lot!

At first it was brilliant, loads turned up, coaches, mini buses, bikes, skateboards. But we didn't reckon on getting hi-jacked. Rent-a-mob turned up, you know the sort. Jump on anyone's bandwagon just to cause a bit of aggro. We wanted it to stay peaceful but this scruffy crowd of layabouts had other ideas. Jackie Corkhill yelled at them to do one but they wouldn't budge. Things started to get really heavy. The bizzies brought in reinforcements.

The whole thing started to back-fire. The prison thought the only way to cool it all was to move the girls to another prison. Mandy and Beth . . . and my baby, moved to the back of beyond.

As the van was leaving the prison, rent-a-mob rushed forward, battering on the side. It was a right mess. The police had had enough and moved in. Poor old Rosie Banks got caught up in it all. No one really knows if that caused it, but a week later I heard she'd lost the baby. I felt dead sorry for her and Eddie. I know how I'd have felt if that had happened to Mandy.

I think they'd decided to move the girls on purpose to the most awkward place in the country for me to get to. Somewhere in the middle of nowhere, otherwise known as Yorkshire. It may as well have been the moon. Why didn't I get a job years ago as a long distance lorry driver . . . or Damon Hill's team mate? At least the I'd have me own set of wheels. But no, I had to be different and opt for the honourable profession of Glazed Cleansing Operative.

So I had to get all kinds of buses and trains just to spend a few grabbed minutes with Mandy and Beth. That's why I was so made up and jumped at the chance when Bing offered me a lift in his pride and joy - his antique Cortina.

Unfortunately it turned out to be a cracked antique and we ended up being towed to the nearest Bed and Breakfast. It's funny, whenever I go anywhere with Bing we end up having to spend the night together - I hope people don't start talking, besides, he's not my type. I hate men with moustaches . . .

Back on the close, Bing and Jean had

Jackie Corkhill was always in the thick of the fight. Jimmy was proud.

troubles of their own. Rachel, it turns out, started acting a bit funny. It seemed she was trying to tell them something. Something from the past about her Dad, Trevor. But every time they got close to her opening up, she clammed up again.

But then Bing hit the jackpot. He was just 'casually' looking (well, alright snooping) around Rachel's room and found a load of old letters Rachel had been hiding. They were from Trevor, and well, not to put too fine a point on it, contained stuff that'd make your hair curl - even if your name was Duncan Goodhew. The letters pretty well spelled out just what that pervert Trevor did to Rachel. "their little secret" he called it - I know what I'd call it.

This was just the break we needed to help the girls' appeal. Bing and Jean worked on Rachel, and thankfully she broke down and told all - she had lied in court. I was almost organising Mandy and Beth's homecoming party.

But Alison, the Solicitor brought me down to earth with a bump. The letters and Rachel's evidence could be the magic key, but it was still going to be tough, especially for Beth. Apparently it would be easier now to show how Mandy was provoked to kill Trevor. 'cause of what he did to Rachel, but Beth was another story. She plotted to kill Trevor, with the poison and that provocation would be difficult to prove for her.

Beth was gutted. It was the night before the appeal, she told her mum she couldn't face coming back to prison alone, she was really down, like Mandy had never seen before. Beth said she'd do anything to not go back to jail.

They were the last words Mandy ever heard from her daughter. I still can't believe it. Next morning two hours before the appeal, the appeal to release them, Beth was dead. Just like that. She came so close to freedom. At first Mandy and me feared the worst. Surely Beth wouldn't harm herself. Not Beth . . .

We got the post mortem report a few days later, Hypertrophic Cardiomyopathy it said. Not that I could understand or even say it.

It was mumbo-jumbo for a heart disease. Common amongst younger people they said. Well, I'd never heard of it. Well, there was that case a few years ago of a young footballer dropping down dead from it, apparently fit, just like Beth. So maybe it wasn't so uncommon.

But then the real bombshell . . . they said it was hereditary and as there was nothing on Mandy's side of the family, it must have come from only one person - Trevor.

Mandy went off her head - saw it as divine retribution "Even from the grave he got to her" she said "Trevor killed Beth, this was his final revenge."

But even with this tragedy, the appeal had to go on and I talked Mandy into going through with it.

In court Rachel played a blinder. She told the whole truth this time, even the Moustache could see he was beaten.

Never accept a lift in old Bing's old car. It always ends with the car getting a lift.

I still can't fully describe the feeling of standing outside on the steps of the appeal court, and looking up as the humungous doors slowly creaked open. Me, Jackie Corkhill and the rest of the campaign women held their breaths as Alison appeared. It was obvious the verdict had been announced, but which was had it gone? Was my kid gonna be born behind bars?

We peered into the darkness and then suddenly the crowd pushed forward. It was as if we'd just scored in the final five seconds of the F.A. Cup. Up to that moment I still wasn't entirely sure what had happened, but something had and then I saw her, my Mandy, blinking in the sunlight, as if she'd been locked away for a hundred years, it felt like more.

I fought me way through the cheering crowds and bobbies. That first hug, as Mandy started to get used to the fresh taste of freedom, was the best, I felt like I'd never let her go again.

After all that'd happened, after all we'd been through, it was over. It was deffo the strangest courtship I've ever known.

As soon as I think Mandy can handle it and can cope with the loss of Beth we'll get married. Hopefully before the baby's born. Then we can start living a normal life. Well, after the last couple of years, if the little green man land in the back yard and move in next door, that will be normal.

You never know, our luck might be changing and we'll win the big one on the lottery, but it won't change me. honest.

Me & Jackie awaiting the appeal verdict. Time has never gone slower.

Beth Jordache—
a young & tragic life

Campaigning Crusaders

The Campaign to get the girls out of jail divided Brookside Close. I was a bit dubious meself at first, wondering whether it was best to let Alison the solicitor get on with it in a legal way, like. But Alison said a lot of public attention could do some good, so I changed my mind.

But there were times when I felt Mandy and Beth were being turned into freaks as various extreme women's groups joined in the battle. I didn't want the world to see the girls as martyrs. Just as ordinary women who'd been driven to killing a maniac to protect themselves. I didn't feel we were fighting for all women, just Mandy and Beth, but sometimes that's how it looked in the newspapers and on the telly.

It all got sort of political, which is not how I saw it at all. I just wanted my girls out of chokey.

Ron Dixon was one of the first to come out against the campaign. He said the Jordache women had been ~~convicted~~ convicted in a court of law and that was that. When his son Mike put up a Free the Jordaches poster in his bedroom window Ron tried to get him to take it down. Mike told him to visit a taxidermist.

All kinds of groups jumped on our bandwagon.

Jackie Corkhill was always in the thick of the fight.

And daughter Jacqui Dixon said she'd never campaign for Beth Jordache but there were personal reasons for that.

The real heart of the Campaign was made up of three women: Patricia Farnham, Jean Crosbie and Jackie Corkhill. At first the other two weren't so sure about Jackie.

I think they reckoned she might be a bit, well .... strident was the word Pat used.

In fact Jackie's straight speaking had a lot to do with the Campaign's success.

Patricia ran the publicity sub-committee, which in fact was the Campaign.

She ordered the Free the Jordaches posters, me and Jean put a lot of them up. Max Farnham was always trying to get Pat to give it up. She was spending too much time on the Campaign, not enough in the gift shop and with the kids. That sort of thing.

Of course they were having money worries at the time. But I've noticed with yuppies that their money worries are different to anyone else's. I mean, it's never about not being able to pay the gas bill, is it? More like God we'll have to put off changing the Mercedes!

Max went too far, though, when he refused to sign the petition to get the girls out. I despised him for that, but then I despise him for all sorts of reasons. It's a hobby of mine.

I was doing me bit, of course. I painted a big banner FREE THE JORDACHES! and hung it on the Gyratory Walkway in town.

Mick said I could get nicked for it, but I didn't care. In a way I'd have almost welcomed a tap on the shoulder from a bizzie. It would have made me feel I was suffering just a fraction of what the girls were going through.

I got a bit worried about the way the papers and the telly seemed to twist everything any of us said. It never came out the way it was said. Jean and Pat said not to worry: all publicity is good publicity sort of thing, but I wasn't so sure.

Pat, Jackie and Jean got very enthusiastic one afternoon about the Campaign and about some champagne. They were drinking the old fizzo and sorting out the bizzo of getting the girls out at the same time.

Max wasn't well pleased, of course, but I understood how they felt. Funny thing was, I seldom felt like a bevvy meself in those worrying days.

An artist likes his work hung. I hung my banner on the Gyratory walkway.

Patrician Pat expected to do the talking, but it was canny Corkhill who really impressed Michael Parkinson when she told the world about the Brookside Two.

Anyway I heard Max had another go at Pat. All she cared about was Mandy and Beth when she should be applying herself to business.

Jean and Jackie had a secret plan they wouldn't tell any of us about. But they reckoned it would make the papers. They went to visit Mandy and Beth in jail and when it was time to end the visit they got out some nylon cable.

Mandy and Beth were mystified but soon saw what was going on. Jackie and Jean tied all four of them together with the nylon stuff. They told the guard they weren't leaving till they got justice for the Jordaches. Brilliant!

Jackie and me took on the full might of the law when they moved Mandy & Beth. Trouble is, we had to cope with Rent-a-Mob too.

Of course it was simple enough for the screws to untangle them and bundle Jean and Jackie out. But the Press had been warned and were waiting outside to snap the two J's.

So were Jimmy and Bing, called by the bizzies to come and collect their trouble-making wives.

Jimmy was chuffed at all the attention Jackie was getting. "Good on yer, girl!" he said. But Bing was mortified. He didn't think any wife of his should behave like that.

But the real highspot of the Campaign was when Jackie, Jean and Pat went on telly to debate what they called the Jordache Issue. Patricia said some sensible things but Jackie was the star when Jean lost her bottle. The TV people had put up some suit of an MP to say the Jordaches deserved all they got and Jackie really got stuck into him.

"Get into the real world!" she told him. I don't think he'd ever been spoken to like that before.

The interviewer was Michael Parkinson, who I've always thought was great. But I'm sure he found taking on Jackie Corkhill on a par with Emu _and_ Mohammed Ali.

I've still got me t-shirt. "Mandy and Beth Jordache are innocent!" Its gone a bit tight to wear.

Alison explained everything to me later. Mandy's conviction had been reduced to manslaughter, which meant that she was let out on probation.

After all that, they decided she was now right to have defended herself and her daughters.

Why couldn't they have just done that at the start? Maybe Beth would still be alive.

Mandy gave this brilliant speech to the press, saying how she was gonna fight on, and establish a women's refuge in Beth's name.

So that Beth's death would not be totally in vain.

Scams, Cons & Trickery

I've changed a lot in the ten years I've been living and working round Brookside. I suppose you could say now I'm one of the good guys. A pillar of the community, like. Though Jimmy Corkhill says that should be pillow of the community. Or even pillock. The cheeky ....

But, to be honest, I haven't always been so respectable. What? I hear you gasp .... Sinbad the villain? Well, no, not a criminal, exactly, like Barry Grant for instance, or Jimmy himself on occasion. But I did, on occasion, used to get involved in the odd scam or entrepreneurial money making venture. Put it this way: if I ~~say~~ saw a bizzie I'd walk the other way. Fast.

I didn't have a lot of choice sometimes. It was a question of making a few bob on the edge of the law or going hungry. And I've never been one to suffer in the food and drink department.

I used to put bets on for people. If they won they'd give me a quid for me trouble. Now where's the harm in that? But there was a time when some woman asked me to put a bet on for her and I knew the horse had no chance. So I just kept her stake in my pocket and never went near the bookie's. Of course the nag did win and I tried to get out of it by saying I didn't get to the betting shop in time for the off, which was true in a way. But pressure, as you might say, was exerted and I had to find the winnings out of me own pocket. I always thought that was a bit unfair, but it taught me a big lesson. That if gambling is a mug's game so is not gambling in certain circumstances.

Met Trevor the turkey, one of the few who enjoyed a happy Xmas.

My most famous scams all had to do with Christmas, season of goodwill to all men except Sinbad. I had this idea of offering fresh turkeys in the Close, cheaper than the supermarket frozen. Just my service to the community. This was before we had the local shopping parade. Collected the money in advance from old man Harry Cross, the Grants, the Nurses and the Collinses. All these used to live on the Close ages ago.

All I actually had was one turkey and he was really fresh - problem was he was so fresh, he was still alive. I called him Trevor and we got on well. Although the next Trevor I met didn't fare as well. I figured that if I turned up on the doorstep with Trevor all alive and trusting, no-one would have the heart to have him topped. Once they'd seen the expression on his face, I thought, they couldn't transfer him to a roasting tin. And in those circumstances they could hardly ask for a refund. So both me and Trev would be the winners.

That was the theory and it worked until I got to Harry's house. Now Harry Cross was a right miserable old skin flint. He grabbed Trevor and called out for a big knife.

Disappeared with the poor bird making bloodthirsty noises. I was expecting the worst but luckily Trevor reappeared still waddling. I didn't make a kid's gold-wrapped Christmas chocolate penny from that one, but Trevor survived to gobble another day and all Harry's lodger Ralph ended up with was a cut finger.

Another year, Jimmy Corkhill was involved with me in the Santa's Sleigh saga. Max Farnham the yuppy bloke, had moved into Number 7 and had joined the Round Table because he thought it would do him a bit of good.

They put him in charge of the Christmas Sleigh, that was supposed to be towed round town collecting for charity.

Now call him ~~maxiev~~ naive, call him foolish, but he left it outside his house and Jimmy and I just borrowed it for a collection of our own. Now where's the harm in that? Jim was Daddy Crimbo in the full red and white gear and I was Santa's little elf in a costume as green as a shamrock. We must have looked a right pair.

We rattled our buckets and took in the cash and Max went spare when he realised he'd have to confess to his posh mates that he'd lost the sleigh. He should have just blamed it on Rudolph or someone.

Eventually we brought it back and hitched it to a lamp-post outside his house. It was the charitable thing to do, and after all it was Christmas. Unfortunately it all back fired and Maxie caught up with us with our buckets brimming over with dosh - we had to hand the lot over. Well, we intended that all along - honest.

Another festive fraud I attempted was to get a load of old Remembrance Day poppies and make them into Christmas decorations. Tried to sell them around the Close but the residents remembered what poppies were all about and I was almost run out of town. I still don't see what the fuss was about. Red and green are the Christmas colours aren't they? And red poppies have green leaves. And Christmas is a time for remembering, isn't it? So what's wrong with Remembrance Day Christmas poppies?

I had another nice little Christmas scam going when I decided that Pick Your Own was the way to get into the Christmas tree trade. Found a plantation of trees that unfortunately belonged to someone else and was about to harvest a nice little crop when the forest ranger turned up and escorted me out of the woods before you could shout TIMBER! I felt like Yogi Bear being nabbed with a load of picnic hampers.

I hadn't been around the close for long when I persuaded Barry Grant to come in with me for a load of ever so slightly dodgy cuddly seals. We sold them right enough – Harry Cross took 30, thinking he'd make a profit selling them on. But then Rommel, a yappy Yorky owned by old Ralph Hardwick, chewed one of them and died.

They were poisonous! The fur was toxic. Just my luck. A broken seal.

Barry and I eventually managed to get them all back – though that involved breaking into a warehouse owned by a well known local gangster and impersonating bizzies – before we dumped the sodding seals on a safe chemical dump. I like to do my bit for the environment. Even thought about joining Green Peace after that.

And I did get Ralph a puppy to replace Rommel.

Nowadays I'm a man of property – came into a nice inheritance off me Mum. But a few years ago things were different. I was homeless and I ended up squatting with Jimmy Corkhill in Caroline Choi's house. I was hopelessly in love with Caroline. She lived at Number 7 and when she went back to Hong Kong after a criminal boyfriend had robbed her blind I was heartbroken. But since her brother Dr Michael Choi was leaving too – he was going to America – I sneaked the back door key and moved in secretly with Jim. Then I went and got made official caretaker of the place!

Sometimes the residents round here start to make their own cutbacks, and often the first casualty is the window cleaner. They think they can do it themselves. The cheek!

It takes years to get to my level. Anyway, when this happens, I need to do a bit of subtle coaxing to start them pleading for my services again.

So once, I threw a load of old tyres onto an old skip in the middle of the close.

Set a light to it, and watched the thick black smoke cover every window of the close — brilliant!

Only problem was the skip got so hot it melted the tarmac and stuck to the road.

I made a sharp exit...

Me & one of the few turkeys who enjoyed a Happy Christmas.

Santa + his favourite little elf, working for the underprivileged. Us!

I was supposed to be helping the Chois sell the house but every time a buyer turned up I'd say the roof leaked or something or the rising damp was in danger of drowning the death watch beetles unless the dry rot got them first.

Alright, a little dishonest, maybe, okay, but it kept a roof over me head for some time. Eventually me and Jimmy got evicted and the Farnhams moved in. I was homeless again and those days they didn't even have the big issue to sell. I stayed in various people's garages and then ended up living in the Collins' garden shed. I accidentally set fire to it with me cooking equipment, a primus stove. Everyone thought I'd been cremated with the shed and one or two weren't that sorry, to be honest, but I'd actually spent the night of the fire elsewhere, thank goodness. Up until then things at Chez Shed were going okay. I survived mainly by changing people's milk orders and then helping meself to the extra gear.

ROLLE' LAST
Local & Alive
FOR SALE
including Rising Damp, Death Watch
beetle, Dry Rot, Large Garden
(subject to subsidence.) Call
Sinbad for appointment to view
at your own risk.

I did me best to keep buyers away!

In me time, I've nicked tiles from a roof then asked the owner if he'd like me to mend it for him. With his own tiles – though he didn't know that. I just thought of it as recycling.

I've flogged fire-damaged wallpaper and pretended the charred effect was part of the pattern. I've even managed to sell flood damaged fireworks – now that took some doing!

I got caught pinching food from the Collins' home freezer and was blackmailed into free window cleaning as a punishment by their cleaner. I've buried a dodgy TV set in Number 9's back garden and then seen it rise from the grave like Dracula. Felt like driving a stake through its screen. Bit like Trevor in the garden next door.

The truth is I just did what I had to do to keep going.
Like most of us.
But now I'm honest.
Honest.

10 STEPS TO THE PERFECT PATIO

Although I have two main professions, window-cleaning and caretaking, I've been known to turn me hand to all kinds of things if the occasions arises. A bit of decorating, a bit of building work, to name a couple.

When I decided Mandy Jordache desperately was in need of a patio in her back garden at Number 10 I knew just how to set about it, because I've laid a few flags in me time, labouring for professional paviors, like.

It's a useful thing, a patio. Gives you somewhere nice and dry to sit out, if the weather's a bit funny. And it can improve the look of a poorly laid out backyard, no end. Covers a multitude of sins, a patio. And it can make your house more attractive to buyers if you want to sell. When Mandy and I put our house on the market all kinds of people turned up, just to look at the patio. They came from far and wide just to view me handiwork. I reckon mine was dead good so if you want some advice, here's ten tips for building the perfect patio.

1. Decide on the size. It needs to be big enough to set a few garden chairs on and to cover any little imperfections under the ground.

2. Using string and pegs mark out the area.

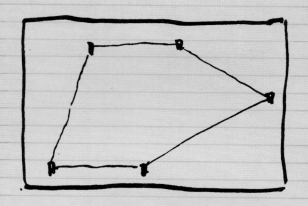

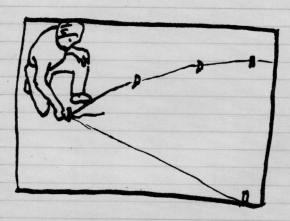

3. Lay a good foundation. This is dead important. You need real body in your foundation. A couple of inches of crushed rubble, well battered down, with an inch of boiler ash or sand on top is usual. Though you can use all kinds of rubbish underneath. But you want it well bedded down, in case it suddenly pops up again – giving you all kinds of problems.

a heavy bit of timber is great for levelling hardcore

Trevor helped with the foundations.

6. Get your final surface well tamped down and level. You don't want it coming up in a hurry.

a long piece of wood is perfect for levelling concrete

Pour the concrete in from the corners

4. Get some help. Beth Jordache actually helped lay the foundations of my patio, though she didn't know it at the time.

5. Decide on which surface you fancy. You can use brick, heavy tiles, stone flags or ordinary concrete flags. And if you drop some by accident – you've got crazy paving! These can sometimes be obtained from your local council building yard. In fact Jimmy Corkhill offered to obtain a few for me, though I'm not sure if he meant to pay for them.

7. You can just lay a square of concrete, of course, though this looks a bit crude. If you do this, roughen the surface with a hard broom or rake when the concrete is nearly dry. This will keep you from slipping up in wet weather. And you don't want any slip-ups with your patio, like I had.

8. Make sure you don't disturb any water wipes when you're preparing your patio because if you damage one this can lead to unfortunate legal consequences. My patio was self-watering. In fact it even watered the garden next door, producing a pretty artificial lake.

9. Decide which plants you want to decorate your patio. You can get various tasteful shrub tubs. The urn-shaped ones are often suitable. Or you can leave out the odd flagstone and plant things directly in the earth. Those standard rose bushes you see in the Gardens of Remembrance at crematoriums are nice.

10. Invite your neighbours round to inspect your new patio, but don't bore the jacksie off them with tales of all the hard work you put into the foundations. They don't have to know what's underneath.

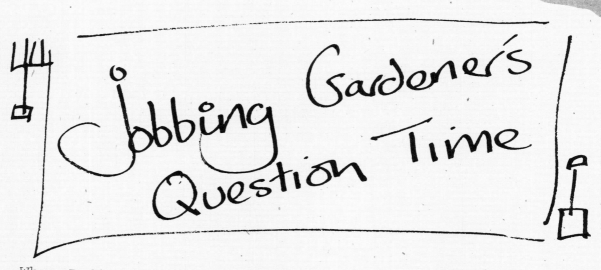

Jobbing Gardener's Question Time

When I first came to Brookside I was more interested in getting on than getting honest. I did a bit of this and that to earn a crust, ducking and diving, making a quid or two where I could.

At one time my reputation was so bad I was run out of town. Run out of the Close, anyway. All because I'd run out of excuses.

It's important to work at a controlled rate and not overtax your strength.

One of me nice little earners on the side was gardening. I didn't know anything about gardens - I could just about tell a turnip from a tulip - me fingers were more a light shade of brown, than green.

I sort of let people think I knew more than I did. I said things like "The soil's in good heart" or "It's all down to the ph value."

I didn't know what it meant either, just a phrase I'd once seen in a newspaper. But nobody actually <u>likes</u> the hard work of gardening. They might pop in the odd daffodil bulb, like, but real sweat isn't that attractive to them. So there were people around who employed me to do it for them.

This little item is just a bit of good advice to any young lad (or laddess) thinking of setting up as a jobbing gardener with or without the knowledge of the Social.

These are valuable tips on how to make some dosh without actually overworking.

Q. What does the customer want from the jobbing gardener?

A. The customer wants a show - wants his/her garden to look very different when you've finished work. That way they feel they're getting value for money. What impresses the customer most is an expanse of bare, weedfree earth. To give this impression simply turn the soil over with a fork and rake out any little baby bits of weed you can see. Underneath the big daddy weeds will be chuckling. They can get growing again with no-one noticing. But the client doesn't know this. And when the weeds do come back so will you. What they call a repeat order. A hardy perennial. If it's pruning that's required prune fiercely. Take a lot off. It may not be too good for the plant but for some reason people think really savage pruning is the mark of the pro. And it's easier to saw off a few main branches than fiddle about with a ton of twigs.

Q. Mowing lawns is hard work. Any advice?
A. If you're forced to cut grass leave the grassbox off, saves emptying it. If the customer complains say it's important to leave the cuttings on the lawn. "Giving the nitrogen back to the soil." But pick your customer. I tried this with Heather Black once (she used to live at Number 9) and she made me sweep up every last blade with a dustpan and brush that must have come from a doll's house. And try not to break anyone's mower. I broke Billy Corkhill's once and the Corkhills are like elephants – they never forget .... or forgive.

Q. If I'm asked to plant shrubs which kinds should I suggest?
A. Always advise evergreens. No leaves to sweep up come the autumn and an old gardener in the local park once told me evergreens discourage weeds growing around them. They take the nourishment out of the soil 365 days a year so weeds go hungry, like. Slow-growing shrubs will cut down on your work considerably. Stay away from anything like Russian Vine which grows so fast you have to jump back once you've planted it and requires a lot of snipping. Holly's a good bet, it grows very slowly. In fact if you grow from seed it takes two years <u>to germinate.</u> Always say holly should be pruned at Christmastime. You can sell what you chop off. Always offer to get the plants yourself from the garden centre, to save the customer trouble. You can often improve the price on the label. Or write a new label. Not that I'd ever stoop so low, of course ....

Q. Are there any free sources of useful plants?
A. Yes, cuttings from other plants – from friends and neighbours. Of course Jimmy Corkhill also reckons on other people's gardens and public parks. He says they're best harvested after dark. Take a spade and a black sack and if questioned by the bizzies say you're doing your bit to Keep Britain Tidy by ridding the hedgerows of weeds.

Q. How much can I charge?
A. Whatever you can get away with. Posh gardeners who arrive in smart vans and wheel out loads of shiny stainless steel tools and fancy machines get seven or eight quid an hour. But most people won't pay much more than four quid for an ordinary bloke, with a cart. Creative timekeeping can help, though. Turn up at half-past three and leave at twenty to six and say

you've done four hours. Most people can't be bothered to tot it up. An exception to that was Harry Cross (again!), who timed you with a stopwatch and would have used Olympic equipment if he could have got his hands on it.

Q. Should I work alone or take on help?
A. Help, but only if it's free. You might be able to persuade a strong young kid to do most of the work for a few cans of Coke and a promise of a few bob tomorrow. Everyone knows tomorrow never comes. I needed Jimmy Corkhill's help to plant a dicey Christmas tree outside the Farnhams once. But since it was meant for a children's home we had to dig it up and replant it there. The wages of dishonesty is hard graft.

Jimmy + me + a Christmas tree. It gave us the right needle.

Sinbad's Tours

We get a lot of tourists in Liverpool. Americans, Japanese, Germans, Swedes, Turnips .... you name it.

Mostly they want to see where the Beatles began. Us Scousers are in two minds about the Fab Four. We're proud of the lads, of course, but we do have this feeling that the world ought to know there's more to this old city than She Loves You, Yeah, Yeah, Yeah.

Now, I must admit, I used to have a bit of a doze during history lessons, but I like to spend the odd hour or two reading up on things in the local library. You know, expand me brain as well as me horizons. You discover some fascinating facts .... like that this old place was here well before the Saxons, Vikings and other assorted scallies. And of course, as everyone knows, Liverpool was once the greatest port in the world.

There's a statue of Christopher Columbus in Sefton Park and underneath it's written The Discoverer of America was the Maker of Liverpool. What it means is that most of the emigrants to Yankeeland went on ships from the Mersey. The Irish, Germans, Italians, the Poles all had to get here before setting off for the US of A. Makes you think, that. Something I'd sooner not think about is all the African slaves that went too, to pick their rotten cotton.

I knew a Pole once, actually .... no, not the type with a flag on top. She was the Farnham's second nanny, went out with my old mate Terry Sullivan. Wonder what happened to her?

Anyway that's how my town got to be this monster port. That and exporting all the stuff Britain started making a couple of hundred years ago. The Industrial Revolution. Eddie Banks, from number nine, he's a bit of an expert on this .... strong union man .... he'll tell you all about it.

ferry cross the Mersey o one of the world's best-known skylines.

The plan they give tourists. I found it useful myself.

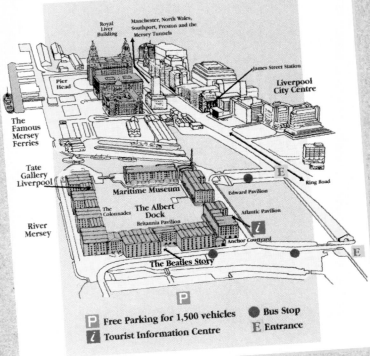

Royal Liver Building

Manchester, North Wales, Southport, Preston and the Mersey Tunnels

James Street Station

Liverpool City Centre

Pier Head

The Famous Mersey Ferries

Tate Gallery Liverpool

Maritime Museum

Edward Pavilion

E

Ring Road

River Mersey

The Colonnades

The Albert Dock

Atlantic Pavilion

Britannia Pavilion

Anchor Courtyard

i

The Beatles Story

E

P

P Free Parking for 1,500 vehicles

Bus Stop

i Tourist Information Centre

E Entrance

I'm not acquainted with the North or the South Pole. The only Pole I know is Anna Wolska, the Farnhams' No.2 nanny.

But I suppose you want to know about the Beatles. I reckon I was about two when Lennon and Macca started messing about with their guitars in John's auntie's front room, but I knew all about them when they started having all those Number One hits. Every six-year-old did. The Cavern, the club they used to play in, is still there .... well sort of .... They tore it down and then used some of the same bricks to build it exactly the same.

The only difference is you can breathe in there now. There's cynical fellers who'll tell you the original screaming girl fans weren't screaming at all. Just gasping for air. They also sold some of the bricks as souvenirs ... Jimmy Corkhill did a raging trade selling his own "Genuine Originals" – funny that, they bore an uncanny resemblance to the knock-off ones he built the Corkhill's garage with.

There's statues all over Liverpool, and the Beatles are no exception. There's a statue to the lads and another one of a lonely old girl sitting on a bench, that's called Eleanor Rigby. Some Southerner called Tommy Steele made it. Charged the city half a sixpence for it, could have been worse – could have been a little white bull!

You can go on bus rides that show you the houses where John, Paul, George and Ringo lived, but they look just like houses to me. You can even go on a Magical Mystery Tour. I've got a mate who lives just off Penny Lane. Always having his picture taken with Japanese tourists. Tells them he's Ringo's third cousin, twice removed.

What I like to remember is something a friend of Lennon once said: "If you look at anyone from Liverpool who's made it, it's partly because <u>they came from Liverpool.</u>"

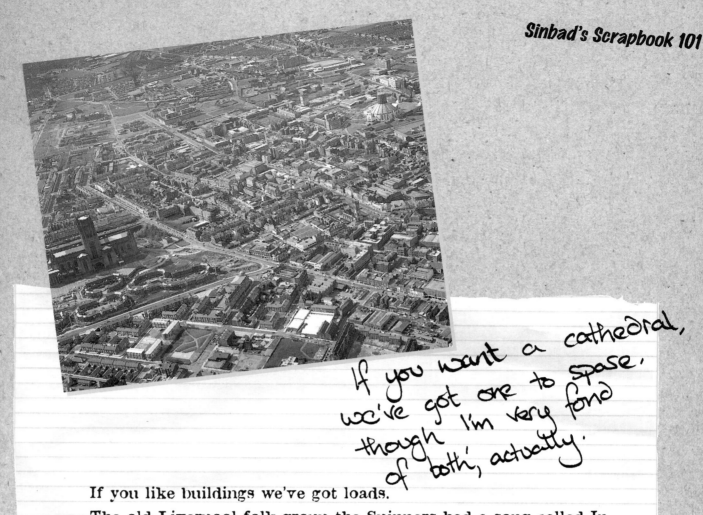

If you want a cathedral, we've got one to spare, though I'm very fond of both, actually.

If you like buildings we've got loads.

The old Liverpool folk group the Spinners had a song called In My Liverpool Home with a line that went like this: "If you want a cathedral we've got one to spare." At this point the singer always used to shout TWO! which pleased the irreligious in the audience.

What they were on about was the Anglican Cathedral – biggest in the country – and the Catholic one. The Anglican building looks really ancient, though I think they only started building it in 1904. Took them years to complete .... they were still building it after I was born .... must have been all the tea breaks.

The Catholic cathedral's a lot more modern and futuristic. I have heard it called Paddy's Wigwam, 'cause of it's weird shape. Looks more like a spaceship to me.

Then there's St George's Hall, where me and Mick Johnson stood on the steps as the only men in a candlelit vigil for Mandy and Beth. That used to be both a Crown Court and a concert hall for big orchestras. Music to sweat in the dock by, like.

There's the ancient Town Hall. If you kneel down in the right spot you can see a plaque over the door to the vaults that tells you during the last war all of Britain's gold reserves were stored there before being sent to Canada for safety.

Two hundred and eight tons of it — enough to keep Mr T in chains for a good six months. Just as well Barry Grant wasn't around at the time.

Down by the port there's some brill buildings. The Liverpool skyline is just as famous as New York's or San Francisco's, you know. The structure everyone knows is the Liver Building with the two mythical Liver birds on top.

They're supposed to flap their wings if a virgin passes by. Ron Dixon claims to have spent half a day watching them through binoculars as 492 girls walked underneath. Didn't see a flutter. But then he's a cynical feller, Ron. He probably had the binoculars trained on the girls, anyway, knowing him.

The docks and dockers hardly exist anymore. Container ships come in, dump these monster crates, take on some more and leave the same day. There's no romance in it.

But the famous Albert Dock has been turned into what they call a cultural complex and it's ace. (They say it's the biggest group of Grade I listed buildings in the country, which must be good.) Anyway there's museums and entertainments and some great sources of scran. And our own Tate Gallery, though I did have to explain to Jim that it wasn't an exhibition of sugar bags. It's all modern art stuff, see. I quite like some of it, well the stuff that makes sense. Me and Jimmy got thrown out once though. We only went in for a cup of tea. For a laugh, Jimmy took off his tatty old training shoes and left them in the exhibition hall with a sign "Lace me up before you go-go". How did we know the security guard had no sense of humour?

Jimmy had some explaining to do to his Jackie when he got home barefooted!

The best way to see the Liverpool skyline is from one of the ferries that link Liverpool to Wallasey and Birkenhead. You can go over humming Ferry Cross the Mersey if you want. Keep an eye out for Gerry Marsden – you never know.

Wallasey's the only word in the language that rhymes with policy. Just thought you'd like to know that. And Birkenhead's interesting because the world's first public park was put there. That feller Joseph Paxton who built the big greenhouse for Queen Victoria – the Crystal Palace – designed it. And they copied Birkenhead Park when they laid out Central Park in New York.

It's funny to sit watching a film on telly and see Jane Fonda or someone doing romantic things in Central Park and then to think it all started just across our river. Wonder why they never named Birkenhead twice – Frank Sinatra could have sang about it then.

There's loads more to tell but I'm getting writer's cramp and me biro's running out.

But I must tell you about the world's first train accident, a few miles from the centre of town at a place called Rainhill. They were racing steam locomotives in 1829 and Stephenson's Rocket won.

But it knocked down a feller called William Huskisson. People weren't used to dodging trains in those days. All these years later, and you wait hours just to dodge one.

Old Bill Huskisson was MP for Liverpool at the time. Lucky it was no-one important. And it's probably the only by-election ever caused by a train running on time.

The fall of Max Farnham (that wasn't)

As you know the Dixons and the Farnhams have been feuding since they both came to Brookside. Ron's always trying to outdo yuppy Maxie's doings and of course, Max is just as bad, getting wound up so easily by Dicko's antics.

I never thought it would turn into a duel, though. Which is what the bungee battle amounted to. Max found himself being volunteered into doing a charity bungee jump. He asked Ron to sponsor him for it, and of course Ron, trying to impress Bev, said he'd do it with him! Anything you can do I can do dafter, sort of thing.

Bev tried to talk Ron out of it, not right for a bloke his age, but that just made him even keener to take the dive. He'd known for some time that restless Bev thought if he wasn't over the hill he was approaching the summit.

He'd been refused entrance to a nightclub for being too close to his bus pass and the bungee jump seemed the only way to prove to Bev he still had what it takes.

What it takes to scare yourself to death, if you ask me, but Ron and Maxie were like a couple of kids taunting each other as Jump Day approached. Max was just as bad. His Patricia said he was stupid for doing it, knowing he even got dizzy climbing the stairs.

Ron Dixon took the fall.

The crane that put the fear into Farnham, Max had no head for heights. No stomach either.

Local Shopkeeper in Bungee Fundraiser

Local shopkeeper Ronald Dixon, 49, (pictured with his partner, 23 year old Beverley McLoughlan), presents a cheque for £200 to neighbours Max and Partricia Farnham for the Alice Farnham Appeal Fund in 1 year old Alice's name in order to raise cash for children with Downs syndrome.

On Tuesday Mr. Dixon did a bungee jump at the local round table fete and collected over £200 in sponsorship money. Afterwards, an exhilarated Mr. Dixon commented, "Although it was my first time, I wasn't nervous at all. I think I must have a head for heights. It was worth it to see the look on the Farnhams' faces."

Local shopkeeper Ronald Dixon, 49, (pictured with his partner, 23 year old Beverley McLoughlan), presents a cheque for £200 to neighbours Max and Partricia Farnham for the Alice Farnham Appeal Fund in 1 year old Alice's name in order to raise cash for children with Downs syndrome.

On Tuesday Mr. Dixon did a bungee jump at the local round table fete and collected over £200 in sponsorship money. Afterwards, an exhilarated Mr. Dixon commented, "Although it was my first time, I wasn't nervous at all. I think I must have a head for heights. It was worth it to see the look on the Farnhams' faces."

Local shopkeeper Ronald Dixon and his partner Beverley McLoughlan present a cheque for £200 to neighbours Max and Patricia Farnham for the Alice Farnham Appeal Fund.

On Tuesday Mr. Dixon did a bungee jump at the local round table fete and collected over £200 in sponsorship money. Afterwards, an exhilarated Mr. Dixon commented, "Although it was my first time, I wasn't nervous at all. I think I must have a head for heights. It was worth it to see the look on the Farnhams' faces." Local shopkeeper Ronald Dixon, 49, (pictured with his partner, 23 year old Beverley McLoughlan), presents a cheque for £200 to neighbours Max and Partricia Farnham for the Alice Farnham Appeal Fund in 1 year old Alice's name in order to raise cash for children with Downs syndrome.

Max and Partricia Farnham for the Alice Farnham Appeal Fund in 1 year old Alice's name in order to raise cash for children with Downs syndrome.

On Tuesday Mr. Dixon did a bungee jump at the local round table fete and collected over £200 in sponsorship money. Afterwards, an exhilarated Mr. Dixon commented, "Although it was my first time, I wasn't nervous at all. I think I must have a head for heights. It was worth it to see the look on the Farnhams' faces." Local shopkeeper Ronald Dixon, 49, (pictured with his partner, 23 year old Beverley McLoughlan), presents a cheque for £200 to neighbours

Local shopkeeper Ronald Dixon, 49, (pictured with his partner, 23 year old Beverley McLoughlan), presents a cheque for £200 to neighbours Max and Partricia Farnham for the Alice Farnham Appeal Fund in 1 year old Alice's name in order to raise cash for children with Downs syndrome.

On Tuesday Mr. Dixon did a bungee jump at the local round table fete and collected over £200 in sponsorship money. Afterwards, an exhilarated Mr. Dixon commented, "Although it was my first time, I wasn't nervous at all. I think I must have a head for heights. It was worth it to see the look on the Farnhams' faces."

When they got to the fete where the bungeeing was going to bungee, they both looked up at this dirty big crane thing and couldn't believe it. Looked like the Eiffel Tower to them and the idea of jumping off it appealed as much as a snog with Cracker the dog.

Anyway, up they clambered and most people thought Ron would lose his bottle for the battle.

But on the platform it was brave young Maxie who couldn't face it and Ron the Grocer who went over the top on his rubber band. Well, this was his chance, wasn't it. Max's bottle having shattered, no <u>way</u> could Ron back out as well. So off he went .... Geronimooooooo ....

Bev couldn't believe he'd actually done it and for that matter neither could Ron. After he got over the shock he was strutting about like a dog with two tails. Or two somethings.

Made sure Max was around when the local paper came to take his picture as the conquering bungee hero.

Of course he had to go to La Luz with Bev to celebrate his win and Maxie's fall from grace – if not from the bungee platform.

Old Ronnie thought he was John Travolta, and giving it loads .... Tuesday Night Fever.

But as he thrashed around the dance floor, he suddenly came over all peculiar and collapsed in the bogs.

A touch of angina, they said. Bev turned into Florence Nightingale for a time – a short time – and Ron got fed up with a diet of not much food and no sex at all.

He began to wonder if all this rivalry with Maxie actually <u>was</u> worth it .... maybe they'd both have to find another pastime.

The MADNESS of Jenny Swift

Mick Johnson first met Jenny Swift when he went to see her about Leo's schoolwork. She was his teacher, like. Mick found her a nice, friendly sort of young woman, and when she offered to help Leo with his swimming that seemed okay.

How could she look so sweet and act so crazy?

But he didn't know Jenny was going to turn out to be a nutter, did he? She soon became absolutely obsessed with him. Mick couldn't see anything at all in her. She was just his kid's schoolmarm.

She asked him out for a drink a couple of times and Mick said no politely. Didn't have time, too busy, washing his hair. She never got the message, though, and one day she got Mick back to her flat. He goes the loo, and comes back to find her standing there naked, nude, and with no clothes on as well.

Well, she did have his jacket XXXXX round her shoulders, but that's all.

Embarrassing for him, like, but he made his excuses and left, and next day she apologised and he said forget it and that should have been that.

Except that Jenny started putting it around that she and Mick were engaged. She even arranged a secret engagement

Jenny only had eyes for Mick but they couldn't see he didn't fancy her.

party. Mick blew his top when he turned up, told her to get lost, which she did. In tears.

Next thing you know she's saying it was all a lovers' tiff and they're getting married in September. Mick didn't know what to do. He shut up shop — she used to turn up for a pizza — took the phone off the hook, basically just hid from Jenny.

It was like something out of a scarey movie. I almost expected to find a rabbit in the pan on the stove.

I had troubles of me own at the time - Mandy's appeal was coming up - but I agreed to go for a few days in a caravan by the sea with Mick and his kids.

Give him a break from Jenny the predator...

Except she followed us. I spotted her on the beach and then she turned up at the caravan. When Mick had a go at her she collapsed. Out cold, we had to send for an ambulance. And when Mick went to hospital to see how she was she'd discharged herself. So what kind of collapse was that?

Back home Mick got a solicitor to send a letter telling her to leave him alone but she turned up saying the letter was a bit over the top, wasn't it? Sort of making light of it.

What really gutted Mick was that no-one else believed Jenny was a nutter. She seemed so nice and normal talking to anyone else. So sort of friendly and sincere.

Jenny made a shrine to Mick, then hid it from the law.

But she gave Mick the idea that she was going to do herself in if he didn't want her. And after a few days when she kept dead quiet he started to get worried. What if she'd cut her wrists or something?

So I went with him to her room in a sort of rooming house place. She wasn't around but we went in anyway - you never know - and found it empty. Except for about two dozen pictures of Mick that is, stuck up to make a sort of shrine. And some of his old socks and shirts she'd nicked. Even some of his bin rubbish in a black sack. We came back with a bizzie but by this time Jenny had taken all the shrine stuff down. The copper told Mick it wasn't a crime for a girl to send flowers and chocolates, as far as he knew. Sort of suggested Jenny wasn't a bad looking girl and he should be so lucky. He even asked Mick for her number to ask her out himself!

That was the thing. No-one else apart from me and Mick could see the danger of the woman. To everyone else she was just this kind, nice looking, ordinary teacher.

Jenny told Mick she had a brain tumour — that was lie Number Two Million — and hadn't long to live. She told him on the phone she was really going to harm herself this time, so me and Mick got over there fast.

I stayed down below with the landlady while Mick went up to Jenny's room. I heard him shouting at her then he came out. She followed — and went over the bannister, crashing to the hall below.

The thing is, to the landlady it looked as if Mick had pushed her. I was more worried in case she was dead.

She wasn't, worse luck. Ended up in hozzy with cracked ribs and a few bruises. And shock, though I think it was Mick needed treating for shock. She told Mick she didn't blame him for pushing her over. She must have driven him to it.

Mick was in a terrible state. He knew he hadn't pushed the girl — though God knows he must have felt like doing it. But he didn't know what she'd tell the police.

It didn't look good for him, not with that suspicious landlady.

So he tried to keep Jenny sweet – till a neurologist let him know there was nothing wrong with her. She hadn't got a brain tumour or anything else physically wrong with her.

Jenny admitted this was true but told Mick a tale about having no friends, no family and a mental condition that needed help fast. She should have had a violin. A right little Billy no-mates.

Like a fool Mick suggested counselling, like a bigger fool he said he'd pay for it, and like the world's top divvy he agreed to take her along to the counselling sessions. I think it was Mick needed counselling.

I couldn't take it. I told him he was round more bends than the Amazon and I refused to babysit Leo and Gemma one night when he was supposed to meet Jenny at the counsellor's place.

So he missed her and got an earful from the counsellor for not taking this poor woman's plight seriously!

So what happens next? Jenny is evicted and whose couch does she end up sleeping on?

That's right. Mick Johnson's.

She just wouldn't move out. In the end Gemma asked Mick if Jenny was going to be her new Mummy. By this time Mick had copped with Bev's clubbing friend Janice and that caused even more ructions with Jenny.

She saw Mick and Janice kissing and another mad plot started in her mixed-up brain. Jenny went to see her father – who wasn't dead as she'd told Mick (surprise, surprise) – and lifted a target shooting pistol from him. And some bullets ....

This was all round the time I was planning on getting hitched to Mandy.

The odd couple. In spite of everything, Mick felt responsible

Mick was going to be me best man and we went off on me stag night, came back to his place in the early hours, a bit worse for wear and slumped on the couch.

I slept the night, but it was dead uncomfy. I found out much later I'd been sleeping on her gun, that she'd hidden under one of the cushions!

So anyway, I agree to meet Mick down the Register Office, cause he wants to see Jenny. She was supposed to be finally moving out that day.

I'm down there, stood up, not only by Mandy, but also, me bezzy man. I wondered if it was me aftershave.

Next day, after all the fuss over Brenna, me and Mandy went off on our cancelled "honeymoon". I still hadn't heard from Mick.

A couple of weeks after I came back and heard the full story.

Apparently, as I'm stood waiting for me nuptials, Jenny pulls out a going away present for Mick. Her Dad's gun.

She holds him there for a few days, not really knowing what she wants.

Eventually everyone starts wondering where Mick's got to, so the local bobby makes a call.

P.C. Coban didn't intend to be a hero, but next minute Jenny only shoots him, in the arm.

Of course, within five minutes the place is surrounded; the S.A.S., F.B.I., C.I.D., I.N.X.S. .... the lot ....

And they swooped.

Jenny's banged up now, finally. But Mick still isn't over it. Thinks she'll be let out any day, and come back to get him again.

And I thought I was unlucky with women! Me and Mick are thinking maybe we'd be better settling down together. Purely platonic, like.

That way we could vet each other's prospective girl friends .... and warn the other one to run a mile if it looks dodgy ...!

Sinbad & Mandy - get married (not)

It was a dead funny feeling after Mandy was released. Part of
me wanted to sing and dance (although if you've ever heard me
at the top of me ladder, you'd know Rod Stewart had nothing to
worry about) and celebrate. The other part was treading on egg
shells, in fear of upsetting Mandy. In the end I felt it best
for her to put the past behind her and move on. I mean, when
would be the best time to ask her to marry me? I knew she'd
never really get over losing Beth, so we may as well be
married and I could be there for her.

Besides, the baby was due in a couple of months and I wanted
my kid to have proper parents right from the start.

And so I popped the question. I felt like I'd already asked
her a hundred times, but we'd had more false starts than the
Grand National.

Anyway, true to form, she hummed and harred a bit. Should she
be rushing into another marriage so quick, especially after
Beth and all that, but eventually, the man from Del Amitri, he
say yes!

It was all systems go, we were gonna tie the knot in two weeks
time. I wish I'd joined the scouts when I was a kid, I was so
nervous I could hardly knot me tie.

Of course, Jimmy had to put his tuppence worth in, didn't he?
Although this was more like ten bob's worth. He took over.

Mandy only wanted a quiet affair, even though, inside I wanted
Paddy's wigwam (the Catholic Cathedral.) But I was so made up
with actually getting married I settled happily for Manor Park
Registry Office.

Jimmy thought this was gonna be Charles and Di, take two.
(Although I hoped it would work out better.) He turned up with
top hats, tails, the lot.

He even supplied the wedding cake. The only problem being
instead of "Mandy and Sinbad Forever" inscribed on it, it had

Billy Corkhill marries Sheila Grant. Jim practised his skills stage-managing the wedding.

"Eric and Pauline". He'd got it second hand. Apparently Pauline had discovered Eric was a bit too friendly with Pauline's sister.

"No problem" chirps Jimmy, "we'll just scrape it off and stick Mandy and Sinbad on it ...."

I should have known better than to let him organise things. Not that I remember letting him. He just took over. Said he had experience. Oh, he had that alright.

His brother, Billy, who'd lived at Number 10 before us, was getting married a second time. To the woman across the street, actually, by the name of Sheila Grant. A lovely woman. Someone you'd wish had been your mum.

Anyway, Jimmy went into overdrive on that one, as well. Organised everything, from the marquee in the back yard, to the vol-au-vents. Must have been a hell of a sized lorry <u>that</u> lot fell off.

He even sorted out dinner suits for all the fellas. Although mine looked more like the dog's dinner.

We all lined up in the lounge wearing our duds. We looked like a gang of retired bouncers, who'd seen better days.

Of course, Jimmy, who's always seen himself as some sort of classy gangster, saved himself the best jacket. In white silk, one of those short ones that Matadors wear (I always thought Jimmy was full of bull.)

He said it gave the whole occasion a touch of class. A bit of the old Miami vice. The result was more Dixon of Dock Green.

I must admit though, the do itself wasn't bad at all - plenty of scran and bevvies, and that.

But then I found out why I was invited. Not to have a nose bag and a few scoops. Oh no, I had to stand out on the Close, keeping watch. "For what?" I asked, knowing I'd regret the answer. "Undesirables" said Jimmy.

Apparently, him and his brother, Billy, had been involved in a long standing family feud with a right gang of head-the-balls. He was worried they might turn up today, on Billy's wedding day, to get revenge.

I couldn't believe it. I was hired as some sort of mafia hitman! Suddenly me dicky bow felt very tight.

I made sure I was constantly supplied with enough bevvy to see me through the ordeal. Dutch courage, I suppose. Although I felt more like that little Dutch boy with his finger stuck in the dyke - very vulnerable.

The afternoon wore on, the party got livelier and my eyes were superglued to the entrance of the Close.

It felt like high noon (actually I think it was about quarter to four.) I was standing there like Gary Cooper, wishing I was Henry Cooper, but looking more like Tommy Cooper.

And then, out of nowhere, a stranger rode into town. The man with no name, although I was to find out later that this was a name I'd remember for a long time.

The stranger had A-levels in looking shifty. Yes, I thought. Definitely one of these no-good scallies that Jimmy told me about. I swallowed so loudly the stranger jumped. I'd unnerved him.

He approached. I tensed up. This is it. He started to make his way towards the party. But he deffo wasn't on the invites. This fella even smelt of trouble.

I had no choice did I? I'd seen Brucie in all the Die Hards. I knew I had to make the first move.

I quickly moved in on him, and grabbed his arm. He swung round.

Now, to this very day, I <u>swear</u> he was gonna take a swing at me. Well, at the time, it didn't half look that way.

So I hit him. Well, attempted to, but he was a bit quicker. Well a lot, actually, and fitter.

When I close my eyes, I can still vividly see his fist coming towards me in slow motion.

It connected with me face, and I flew backwards across the bonnet of one of the guests' cars, shouting for help. I'd heard what these guys were capable of, and I've always liked having me kneecaps just where God intended them.

Jimmy and the other penguin suited lads came legging it out of the ~~party~~ party to me aid.

But instead of pulverising this fella and giving me the old hero's treatment, they started laughing. Laughing! With me holding me cut lip!

Over the years I've met the various residents of Brookside Close in many varying ways. But this must have been the most unusual (and painful). How was I to know that Max Farnham would choose today, of all days, to come and look at his new house - Number 7?

And how was I to know that Max could pack quite a punch? Never apologised either. Said it was my fault - the cheek!

That's why I felt quite justified charging him extra when I started doing his windows - just saw it as compensation, like.

So who could blame me for feeling dubious at letting Jimmy organise another wedding - me own? I certainly didn't want a cut lip on all the wedding photies.

But, as usual, there was no telling him. He just carried on anyway. Even when I told him that he wasn't going to be me best man. I'd asked Mick Johno, instead.

I thought it'd shake some sense into Jimmy, to clean his act up. I certainly didn't want a drug dealer as me best man.

So everything was gradually sorted and the big day got nearer. I thought nothing can stop us now.

But then, I hadn't reckoned on the wicked witch of the north-west making her reappearance.

Brenna, Trevor's loving sister and professional trouble maker turns up on our doorstep, with a pitiful look of sorrow and guilt in her eyes.

Told us she was sorry for all she'd said and done. She realised now that Mandy was right to kill her brother. A total turnaround. Said she'd felt like this since Beth's funeral.

From the off, I didn't believe her. People with that much hate can't change. Not so much. Not after all that'd been said.

But Mandy listened. Took it all in and slowly, but surely, started to think that Brenna was sorry and now wanted to be friends.

I wasn't so convinced.

Next, Brenna comes round saying she's lost her job. That she's got no one. With a personality like that, no wonder.

I couldn't believe it when Mandy said that Brenna could move in with us for a while. But Brenna had been trying every trick in the book to wheedle her way in - just like brother Trevor did - must run in the family.

So, for the sake of me upcoming marriage and a bit of peace, I went along with it - reluctantly.

Brenna stirs her witch's brew.

Actually, Brenna <u>had</u> appeared to change. She was as good as gold, always helping with the cleaning and cooking. Especially the cooking ....

About a week to go, and Mandy started to feel a bit sickly. I thought it was down to her being pregnant, Jimmy, always looking on the bright side, said it might be the return of the plague.

I packed her off to the doctors, who said it was just some mild bug, nothing too serious, and to just rest.

We couldn't believe it. Brenna went into Mrs Wonderful overdrive, helping out and caring for Mandy, as best she could.

The big day got nearer, and Mandy got sicker. But she was determined to go through with it.

Come zero hour and there's me, best bib and tucker, new hair cut, looking like Brad Pitt (Snake to my friends) standing waiting at the registry office.

There was only a couple of things missing. Nothing important – only the best man and the bride.

Mick was held up somewhere (I later found out he was held up at the end of a gun!) and Mandy was <u>supposed</u> to be meeting me there.

I should have known something would go wrong. Fate was against us. Only this time it was spelt Brenna.

Back at the house, feeling really sick now, Mandy walks in on Brenna, who was secretly preparing yet another lethal cocktail for her.

Now I don't want to say I told you so, but .... all this
time Trevor's sibling had been trying to kill Mandy, slowly
and surely with her poisonous ways. In revenge for what
Mandy had done to her brother.

There was a bit of a fight, and they both fell down the
stairs. But Brenna's hide was
thicker than a rhino's and she
was off, hoping that the dirty
deal was done.

And so there's me, looking a
right divvy, stood up at the
registry office, not knowing
all this was going on.

There was I, waiting at
the Registry Office.

When I knew she wasn't coming,
we all came back to the Close,
very quietly. Well almost
quietly as we'd been
gatecrashed by Julia Brogan.
Subtle as a mallet, she says
I'm better off out of it — I'd
only be worrying every time
Mandy goes for the cutlery
drawer!

When we get back to the house,
it looked deserted. I didn't have me key, so Eddie Banks
gets his toolbox to help me break in.

Easier said than done, until Jimmy steps forward, and using
his "time honoured skills" has the locked door opened in
seconds.

It was Rachel who found her mum at the bottom of the stairs.

That night was the longest ever waiting in the hospital
corridor.

Thank God Mandy <u>and</u> the baby were alright. I wanted to call
the police, to sort Brenna out once and for all, but Mandy,
ever forgiving, wouldn't hear of it.

She said she didn't want any more trouble, no more police, no more courts, no more nothing.

I could see her point, but I wanted to kill Brenna, myself.

I went out for some coffees, and couldn't believe me eyes when I found Brenna, bold as they come, walking into the hospital.

"Come to finish her off?" I hissed at her. Brenna came back at me with one of her looks. The one that could make milk go off at a hundred yards.

I grabbed her and made sure she realised I meant business. I threatened her with the police and said if they won't do anything then I will. I'd be willing to do time for her if she came anywhere near Mandy or my unborn child, ever again.

I think it worked, in fact I was so convincing I scared myself.

That was the last we saw of Brenna. Let's hope it's forever.

Mandy came out the hozzy next day and I tentatively suggested we rearranged the wedding.

I could tell by her eyes what the answer would be. After this latest palaver, she just couldn't face it yet. I agreed to wait, but we still had our honeymoon booked in the Lake District. We were supposed to be going that day.

I suggested we use it as a much needed holiday, there'd still be time to get hitched before the baby's born, when we get back.

So off we went to the land of the lakes, trying as best we could to put all our worries behind us, and looking forward to the birth of Sinbad Junior. Easier said than done ....

Sinbad, Mandy and Ruth – New Beginnings

We had a brill time up in the Lakes. Even though it wasn't our Honeymoon, at times it felt like it.

Mandy got a bit knackered with all the walking though. Well, who could blame her? Our unborn kid was getting close to making an appearance soon, and if it took after me, she must have been carrying round a hell of a weight.

We got back onto the Close with loads of dirty washing and even more on our minds. I knew Mandy still didn't want to rush into getting married, but we'd finally sold the house to Jimmy, so we had to find somewhere else to hang our hats.

We'd both fallen in love with the Lake District, probably cause it held so many good memories for us. I wanted us to up sticks and find a little cottage up there for us.

I could easily relocate me windows business. I mean, they have windows up there, don't they? And if times got hard, I could easily polish up the odd sheep.

While we debated all this, Jimmy let us lodge in his new house. It was funny suddenly being guests in our own place. But Jimmy and Jackie had firmly put their own stamp on the place. He'd certainly splashed out, but proved that money doesn't necessarily buy good taste. Classy, he called it. It felt like we were living in one of those rave clubs.

It was about two weeks before the baby was due, so I hadn't quite entered panic mode yet.

Just as well, cause there we were doing a bit of shopping in Ron's place, when Mandy's face suddenly went a funny colour. I thought it was wind, but she put me right.

"Sinbad, my waters have broke."

Well, I don't know if it was the shock of Ron's prices or the thought of Jimmy's wall paper, but this was it. I was gonna be a dad, two weeks early. Trust my kid to be punctual.

So me and Ron did what fellas are best at — we panicked. We were very good at it.

I went for the phone, but Mandy shouted there wasn't enough time to wait for an ambulance.

Then Ron came up with his masterstroke. Our own personal ambulance was suddenly on standby, waiting to take us to the hozzy. It was like something out of Thunderbirds — and this was Thunderbird Six — Ron stood there, looking for all the world like Virgil, (without the strings) waiting to transport us at hyperspeed .... well not exactly hyperspeed. More likely at a sedate 40mph, the top speed Ron's moby would allow. Just as well, Mr Tracy had just got it's MOT.

Next minute we're bombing along, with Ron doing his Damon Hill impression and me and Mandy in the back amongst the baked beans and tinned peaches.

And then it happened, or rather it <u>started</u> happening. She was having it, there and then, my baby!

Now my only experience of being a midwife extends to watching westerns where they say — "get plenty of hot water and towels!" I mean, what do you do with them?

So there we are, parked near this bus stop and Ron's doing a roaring trade flogging his wares. The man could put Richard Branson to shame.

And then Ruth turned up. But she wasn't called Ruth then. She was just this pink ball of something you wanted to hold. To protect forever.

My little girl.

I swung open the hatch of the moby, and announced her arrival.

"The baby's had a Mandy."

Alright, I got a bit tongue tied, who wouldn't?

I couldn't have been happier. I don't think I'll ever repeat that feeling, ever.

Me, a Dad, who'd have thought, eh?

A few days later and we brought her back to the Close.

We decided on Ruth Elizabeth as names. Couldn't have been anything else really. Ruth after me mum, and Elizabeth, of course, after Beth.

I didn't know such little things can make so much noise. And how do they know to always do it, just as you're dozing off at two in the morning?

But I didn't care, this was my daughter. She could scream the house down if she liked. Good pair of lungs like her old dad. Probably gonna be an opera singer.

And so, me, Mandy and Ruth continued to look for somewhere to start our new lives together.

Normally, this is where the story should finish, shouldn't it? You know, and they all lived happily ever after. That sort of thing.

But no, this was different. This was Sinbad's life story. Thomas Henry Edward Sweeney. Purveyor of fine windows, loving partner and father of one.

Mandy gets a visit one day, out of the blue, from Mrs Shackleton, the woman who runs the charity refuge for battered wives. It was her who looked after Mandy and the girls and got them the safe house on Brookside Close.

She wanted Mandy to do this talk, to other women in a similar situation. Said they could learn from Mandy's experiences. That she'd become some sort of role model.

Mandy wasn't too fussed at first. Said she'd be too nervous. Had never spoken in public before.

But like a divvy, I talked her into it. I didn't realise then that I was talking her into leaving me.

And baby makes three.
Whoever thought I'd be a Dad?

So the talk went well, very well, and Mandy discovered that she's got more to offer.

She gets involved with a young girl, name of Cathy, and apparently she's getting the life knocked out of her by her husband.

Mandy sees Cathy as being a younger version of herself, even with two young girls. She talks this woman into leaving hubby, and moving into a refuge.

I told her to leave it at that. Leave the past behind, so we could move on. But, of course, Mandy couldn't. She'd found a vocation, hadn't she?

The more I asked her to drop it, the more she got involved.

Next minute, Cathy's irate husband turns up on the doorstep demanding to know where his wife is. I threw him out. But Mrs Shackleton and the charity were really impressed by Mandy's performance and offered her this job in Bristol, living in. Helping organise a refuge for the desperate Cathys and Mandys of this world.

Unfortunately, this being a women's hostel there was no room for the Sinbads of this world.

Right away Mandy dismissed the idea. Said there was no way she could leave me behind, especially now with Ruth.

But I knew Mandy well. Better, I think than anyone else has or ever will. I could see in her eyes that she wanted, no, needed to do that job. And I was being used as the excuse for her not doing it. How'd you think that made me feel?

And so the subject was dropped until Cathy turns up again, battered and bruised, needing Mandy's help.

Mandy looked at me, she even tried to say to Cathy she couldn't help, but in her heart she didn't mean it. So I told her, I actually told her to go, the ultimate sacrifice.

But how could she stay and regret it forever? She'd start to regret me then. This was the only way she could be truly happy. For the first time in her life doing what <u>she</u> wanted to do, not what others tell her to. <u>Her</u> choice, for the first time in her life.

And so I had to let her go. Even I knew you can't hang on to someone using emotional blackmail. It was 5th November when she left. Eddie Banks was having a fireworks party out on the Close. I felt like a damp squib. Even me sparkler wouldn't light.

We said we'd see how things go, and that I'd still see Ruth as much as possible. But they're all the old cliches aren't they? I know Mandy's throwing herself into her new life and job, and hasn't got much time nowadays to see me. I'm not too sure whether I want to see her actually. It's for the best – another cliché – but as long as she's happy and she'll never be hurt again, and of course I'll see our Ruth, whenever I can visit. But it's difficult, I'm busy, aren't I? You know, me window round, looking after the shops, and me bezzy mate, Mick Johno. And you don't have to be with someone all the time to love them. You can do that from anywhere, day or night.

Looking Into the Old Crystal Ball

I don't think I can fit anything else into this scrapbook – it's full to bursting.

But it's served me well. I'm glad I took it up now. It's been more than just a book of old memories. It's me life. Happy and sad. The good, the bad, and Jimmy Corkhill.

I suppose I should think about nipping into Ron's shop and buying a new one – "Sinbad, Volume Two – The Thinning Years".

Or maybe I'll go up market and splash out on a smart one from Pat Farnham's Gift Box. You know, add a dash of style, like.

Whatever I do, I know I'll have plenty to fill it with. Somehow I'm one of those people that stuff happens to. Heavy stuff. And good stuff. But loads of stuff.

Sometimes when I'm up the top of me ladder, doing what I do best, I try to imagine where I'll be in ten years time, what I'll be doing, what I'll look like.

Still a modestly, good looking fella, I should imagine.

And thinner, I hope. 'Cause Mick's put me on this diet, hasn't he? The F-Plan and we all know what that stands for. I just blame it on Cracker the dog.

Our Ruth'll be a teenager, before I know it. I still wish I could have brought her up like a proper dad, but it wasn't to be, was it?

Anyway, just think of all the heartache I'm missing out on - worries about school, and boyfriends, and spots and such like.

You probably know me well enough now to know I'm not a very good fibber. I'd do anything to have all the worries of being a dad - and more!

But I'm old enough and hopefully wise enough to know it'd be impossible for me and Mandy to be together.

I've got some cracking little pictures of Ruth. And just <u>knowing</u> she's mine, always will be, makes me feel good inside. No one can take that away from me.

And I'm gonna get her some brill crimbo pressies. Only the best for my Ruth.

Eh, but don't be feeling sorry for me. I don't want pity or anything. I can look after meself, I can.

Window cleaners have to. It's in their blood. We have to fight through all the elements, shrug off attacks from ferocious animals (well, the odd corgi ...) and extract our fees from some of the most miserly customers on earth. (Have you ever seen Ron Dixon's wallet?) Just to make sure we can hold our heads up and know, proudly, that the windows of the world have been cleaned to perfection. We will fight them on the beaches .... sorry, got a bit carried away the, came over all Churchill like.

So I wonder what the future does hold for me? Julia Brogan said her mate would read me tarot cards for me. But I don't fancy it. Knowing what's gonna happen would take away all that surprise element, wouldn't it?

I mean, if I knew that all that <u>has</u> happened to me, was gonna happen to me, before it happened .... then I wonder if I'd still have gone through with it? Do you follow? I hope so, cause I've no idea what I'm on about.

So let's just hope lady luck's waiting round the corner with some <u>nice</u> surprises for a change. Maybe I'll come up on the lottery like Eddie and Rosie Banks. What would I do with 17 million?

Well, I'd buy a new chamois for a start .... <u>and</u> a gold plated bucket. It won't change me .... honest'

PHIL REDMOND'S

BROOKSIDE
the teenagers

Growing up on The Close - an insiders guide
from the UK's best known teenagers

PG

eth Jordache, Margaret Clemence,
amon Grant, Katie Rogers, Mike Dixon,
acqui Dixon, Sammy Daniels, Owen Daniels

Recorded specially for this video release inside No.5 Brookside Close and featuring Beth, Margaret, Damon Grant, Katie, Mike, Jacqui, Sammy and Owen talking about growing up on The Close. This unique video is packed with specially chosen clips from the first twelve years of the series.

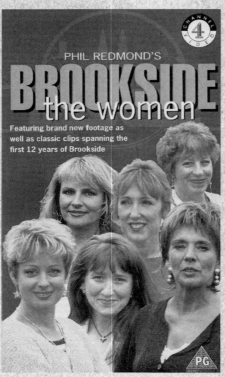

CHANNEL 4 VIDEO

PHIL REDMOND'S

BROOKSIDE
the women

Featuring brand new footage as
well as classic clips spanning the
first 12 years of Brookside

PG

Never seen before on television and filmed in the Farnham's house, you can see Sheila Grant, Patricia, Bev, Sue Sullivan, Mandy and DD chatting with Phil Redmond. This video offers a unique insight into the lives, loves, triumphs and disasters of its females characters. Also features brilliant clips spanning the entire Brookside series.

Both videos are available to buy from your normal video stockist, but you can order direct from Channel 4 Video simply by sending a cheque made payable to BSS for £12.99 (plus £1.50 p&p) to Channel 4 Video, BSS, PO Box 6120, London W5 2GJ